God's Healing Promises

God's
Healing
Promises

Charles ❧ Frances Hunter

🔲 *Whitaker House*

Unless otherwise indicated, all Scripture quotations are taken from the *New King James Version* (NKJV), © 1979, 1980, 1982 by Thomas Nelson, Inc. Used by permission. All rights reserved.

Scripture quotations marked (AMP) are taken from *The Amplified Bible,* Old Testament © 1965, 1987 by the Zondervan Corporation. The Amplified New Testament © 1958, 1987 by The Lockman Foundation. Used by permission.

Scripture quotations marked (TLB) are taken from *The Living Bible,* © 1971 by Tyndale House Publishers, Wheaton, Illinois. Used by permission.

GOD'S HEALING PROMISES

Charles and Frances Hunter
Hunter Ministries
201 McClellan Rd.
Kingwood, TX 77339-2710

ISBN: 0-88368-630-9
Printed in the United States of America
Copyright © 2000 by Charles and Frances Hunter

Whitaker House
30 Hunt Valley Circle
New Kensington, PA 15068

2 3 4 5 6 7 8 9 10 11 12 13 / 08 07 06 05 04 03 02 01

Contents

God's Healing Promises

THE WORD OF GOD is loaded with precious and valid promises about healing, and is exactly like medicine! You need to take enough of it until you are totally and completely healed, and then keep on taking it in maintenance doses. Look upon every verse as another dose of heavenly medicine, and keep on taking doses of divine medication until you are totally and completely healed by the Word of God. This is what God promises, and if God says it, it is true! The Word of God is the best medicine you will ever find, and it's also free! In these days of escalating prescription prices, what a blessing this is!

The single, most important thing to believe is that it is God's will to heal you! Many years ago I used to hear people pray, "If it be Thy will. If it be Thy will." When you study the Word of God from beginning to end, you will understand that His desire is to heal you. From the beginning of the Old Testament, all the way to the end of the New Testament, we will see this fact established.

In order to receive a healing, one must have a foundation upon which to build. Hebrews 13:8 tells us that *"Jesus Christ is the same yesterday, today, and forever."* Therefore, if He healed yesterday, He will heal today and He will heal forever. It is so vital that we believe this in our hearts and not just with our heads, because He has not changed nor will He ever change. Malachi 3:6 says, *"For I am the LORD, I do not change."* We need to remember that what Jesus did from the very beginning, He will do until the very end! We need to establish this in our hearts without any question whatsoever, because it is so critical for us to remember!

We can quote healing Scriptures until we are blue in the face, but until we understand some of the principles of God, it won't bring the healing power we need. Therefore, I want to lay down a foundation for you so that if you need healing, it will be easy for you to receive. The same principle applies to medicine. If the doctor doesn't tell you how to take it, there's no foundation! The medicine won't do what it is supposed to do!

Some of the first Scriptures to become immersed in are the ones that will convince you God wants you well. Read all of these over and over so that you know it is His will to heal. As you read these biblical accounts of healing, let His presence envelop

you and heal you in the process. Read these until they become
a living part of you:

*And Jesus went about all Galilee, teaching in their synagogues, preaching
the gospel of the kingdom, and healing all kinds of sickness and all kinds
of disease among the people. Then His fame went throughout all Syria;
and they brought to Him all sick people who were afflicted with various
diseases and torments, and those who were demon-possessed, epileptics, and
paralytics; and He healed them.* (Matthew 4:23–24)

*[The centurion said,] "Only speak a word, and my servant will be
healed."...[Jesus answered,] "As you have believed, so let it be done for
you." And his servant was healed that same hour.*
(Matthew 8:8, 13)

So He touched her hand, and the fever left her.
(Matthew 8:15)

*When evening had come, they brought to Him many
who were demon-possessed. And He cast out the spirits
with a word, and healed all who were sick.*
(Matthew 8:16)

There met Him two demon-possessed men, coming out of the tombs, exceedingly fierce, so that no one could pass that way. And suddenly they cried out, saying, "What have we to do with You, Jesus, You Son of God? Have You come here to torment us before the time?" Now a good way off from them there was a herd of many swine feeding. So the demons begged Him, saying, "If You cast us out, permit us to go away into the herd of swine." And He said to them, "Go." So when they had come out, they went into the herd of swine. And suddenly the whole herd of swine ran violently down the steep place into the sea, and perished in the water.

(Matthew 8:28–32)

Then behold, they brought to Him a paralytic lying on a bed…. Then He said to the paralytic, "Arise, take up your bed, and go to your house." And he arose and departed to his house.

(Matthew 9:2, 6–7)

Then she came and worshiped Him, saying, "Lord, help me!"…Then Jesus answered and said to her, "O woman, great is your faith! Let it be to you as you desire." And her daughter was healed from that very hour.

(Matthew 15:25, 28)

And when He had come into the house, the blind men came to Him. And Jesus said to them, "Do you believe that I am able to do this?" They said to Him, "Yes, Lord." Then He touched their eyes, saying, "According to your faith let it be to you." And their eyes were opened. (Matthew 9:28–30)

As they went out, behold, they brought to Him a man, mute and demon-possessed. And when the demon was cast out, the mute spoke. (Matthew 9:32–33)

Then Jesus went about all the cities and villages, teaching in their synagogues, preaching the gospel of the kingdom, and healing every sickness and every disease among the people. (Matthew 9:35)

And when he had called His twelve disciples to Him, He gave them power over unclean spirits, to cast them out, and to heal all kinds of sickness and all kinds of disease. (Matthew 10:1)

The blind see and the lame walk; the lepers are cleansed and the deaf hear; the dead are raised up and the poor have the gospel preached to them.
(Matthew 11:5)

Jesus...said, "Be of good cheer, daughter; your faith has made you well." And the woman was made well from that hour. (Matthew 9:22)

Heal the sick, cleanse the lepers, raise the dead, cast out demons. Freely you have received, freely give. (Matthew 10:8)

And behold, there was a man who had a withered hand....Then He said to the man, "Stretch out your hand." And he stretched it out, and it was restored as whole as the other. (Matthew 12:10, 13)

Great multitudes followed Him, and He healed them all. (Matthew 12:15)

Then one was brought to Him who was demon-possessed, blind and mute; and He healed him, so that the blind and mute man both spoke and saw. (Matthew 12:22)

And when Jesus went out He saw a great multitude; and He was moved with compassion for them, and healed their sick. (Matthew 14:14)

❋

Then great multitudes came to Him, having with them the lame, blind, mute, maimed, and many others; and they laid them down at Jesus' feet, and He healed them. (Matthew 15:30)

❋

They...brought to Him all who were sick, and begged Him that they might only touch the hem of His garment. And as many as touched it were made perfectly well. (Matthew 14:35–36)

❋

Now a leper came to Him, imploring Him, kneeling down to Him and saying to Him, "If You are willing, You can make me clean." Then Jesus, moved with compassion, stretched out His hand and touched him, and said to him, "I am willing; be cleansed." As soon as He had spoken, immediately the leprosy left him, and he was cleansed. (Mark 1:40–42)

❋

Most assuredly, I say to you, he who believes in Me, the works that I do he will do also; and greater works than these he will do, because I go to My Father. And whatever you ask in My name, that I will do, that the Father may be glorified in the Son. If you ask anything in My name, I will do it. (John 14:12–14)

❋

Get Rid of Unbelief

It is so vital that we believe that God wants us well. Matthew 13:58 says, *"Now He did not do many mighty works there because of their unbelief."* We need to get all of the unbelief out of our lives as quickly as we can because unbelief can hinder healing, or any other work God desires to do.

God on the Spot

Unbelief is one of the biggest boulders standing in the way of receiving a healing—or in fact any other kind of answer to prayer.

Every so often my "prayer power" is really put on the line by individuals. After my first service at a state camp meeting, a number of ministers and laymen came up to me and said, "Frances, will you pray one of your 'dumb' prayers for us?" Without a moment's hesitation, I replied, "Certainly!"

Then they told me the following story. They were expecting the largest camp meeting they had ever had, and the original well was not big enough to supply the water needs for camp meeting week. To solve the problem, they had drilled a well during the past week and had hit beautiful, clear spring water. Then the Devil came in; a rock had been sucked up into the pipe, which was down 276 feet, and the water was shut off as a result. Two days of intensive working to get the rock out had been to no avail. The well-digging company was coming the next day to take the pipe up, remove the rock, and sink the pipe again at a tremendous expense. They asked me to pray and ask God to remove the rock. I think I groaned inwardly as I said, "Lord, they really put my faith on the spot, don't they?" And I had no more than said this when I realized they weren't putting me on the spot at all; they were putting God on the spot. At this moment Malachi 3:10–11 came to my mind:

🦋

"Bring all the tithes into the storehouse, that there may be food in My house, and try me now in this," says the LORD of hosts, "if I will not open for you the windows of heaven and pour out for you such blessing that there will not be room enough to receive it. And I will rebuke the devourer for your sakes, so that he will not destroy the fruit of your ground, nor shall the vine fail to bear fruit for you in the field," says the LORD of hosts.

🦋

And that's just exactly what I did!

I asked everyone to form a big prayer circle around me so that we could agree in prayer. Then an interesting thought came into my mind that I am sure came directly from the Holy Spirit, because I knew this was so important for the success of the camp meeting. I also knew that it was a tremendously expensive project! I didn't want any unbelievers in that circle whatsoever, so I smiled real sweetly and said, "If there is anyone in this circle who doesn't believe that God is going to get that rock out of there (and then I totally changed my voice and yelled at the top of my lungs), get out of this circle!" Talk about a surprise—I was shocked because 95 percent of the people in the circle, when challenged with unbelief, jumped out of the circle, and I was left with only seven people. I said, "Well, guys, we had better regroup because there aren't very many of us left who really believe." So we joined hands again and I prayed a very simple prayer.

"God, this is Your money. You can spend it to have the pipe taken up and put down again, or You can use it to win souls to Jesus Christ by merely getting the rock out. So I thank You for getting the rock out right now, in the name of Jesus."

One of the pastors left the circle and walked over to the little pump house where the pump was. He turned the pump on, and I instantly heard the most beautiful sound I think I have ever heard in my life! Two hundred and seventy-six feet down in the earth I heard glug, glug, glug—and in a split second the water was shooting out of the well like out of a fire hose! The rock was gone! Praise the Lord![*]

The fabulous thing about God is that we never really understand how He works—we just know that He does.

[*]Account originally published in *Hang Loose with Jesus*, © 1972 by Frances Hunter.

Would God Do It for Me?

It's amazing how miniature our faith is at times and it's thrilling what God will do for us if we will just believe and trust Him!

At about 10 A.M. on a terrible, rainy day, I started driving from Lafayette to Anderson, Indiana, to speak at Purdue University. As I drove along, it was almost impossible to see the road or the cars in front of me. The rain kept getting worse and worse until I was just crawling along at about fifteen miles an hour. The windshield wipers were going full speed, but they still failed to keep the water off the windshield.

After I had traveled three sections of the highway, which were covered with water, I began to panic and decided to find a gas station and call my husband to see if he felt I should go back. But then I said to myself, "That's silly. Charles isn't the one to ask; God is." So I said, "Lord, shall I turn the car around and go back?" Then I believe the Devil got in the car with me and said, "There won't be anyone coming out to hear you in such bad weather. Why don't you go back?"

However, I didn't hear God speaking to me, so I continued. After another three or four miles, I really began to panic because it was almost impossible

to drive. I desperately looked around for a little patch of
blue in the sky when I stopped to fill up with gasoline, but
couldn't see one spot that looked promising. I got back into
the car and started on, and then I began thinking to myself—or
should I say to God?

My conversation went something like this: "God, You couldn't stop
the rain and turn the sky blue, could You?"

The effective, fervent prayer of a righteous man avails much.
(James 5:16)

I looked around again for a little sign of blue sky, but there was
none! Then I continued "thinking to God," and I said, "Now, Lord,
I *know* You could, because the Bible says You parted the Red
Sea. If You could part the Red Sea, then I know that You could
stop the rain and turn the sky blue."

Then the Devil got in the car again (maybe he never
left) and said, "Sure, He could turn the sky blue
and stop the rain, but why should He do that for
you? Who are you?" And I thought, "That's right,
who am I to ask God for something like that?" Then
another thought came into my mind: "Who am I? I'm
God's girl. I'm a child of God. Because I am God's
girl the Bible says I can ask for whatever
I want, and it will be done!" (See
Matthew 21:22.)

So very simply I said, "God, You know I can't see well enough to get through this rain, so would you please stop the rain and make the sky blue?" God's Word says to trust Him, and that's all I did. Within thirty seconds the rain stopped, and within one minute the sky was blue. I drove all the way to Anderson and back to Lafayette on dry highways and under blue skies.

I believe God loves you enough to do this for you, if you will only ask! Whenever I have retold this story in the region where it happened, someone has come up to the microphone to tell the audience that they vividly remember the rain stopping and the sun coming out so suddenly on that particular Thursday. I think it's fabulous how God always lets someone else see the miracles, too!

God is still in the miracle-making business today, just as He was when He stopped the sun and the moon because of the prayer of one man, Joshua.

Then Joshua spoke to the LORD..., and he said in the sight of Israel: "Sun, stand still over Gibeon; and moon, in the Valley of Aijalon." So the sun stood still, and the moon stopped, till the people had revenge upon their enemies....So the sun stood still in the midst of heaven, and did not hasten to go down for about a whole day.
(Joshua 10:12–13)

Let's all start asking more!

Don't Back Down

Once you have determined in your heart that God is going to heal you, and you have meditated on and memorized the Scriptures, and you have read all the stories about healing, let me encourage you not to back down but to stand firm where your faith is concerned. Here are some Scriptures to help you.

God is not a man, that He should lie, nor a son of man, that He should repent. Has He said, and will He not do? Or has He spoken, and will He not make it good? (Numbers 23:19)

Therefore take heart, men, for I believe God that it will be just as it was told me. (Acts 27:25)

Let God be true but every man a liar. As it is written: "That You may be justified in Your words, and may overcome when You are judged." (Romans 3:4)

And not being weak in faith, he did not consider his own body, already dead (since he was about a hundred years old), and the deadness of Sarah's womb. (Romans 4:19)

He did not waver at the promise of God through unbelief, but was strengthened in faith, giving glory to God, and being fully convinced that what He had promised He was also able to perform. (Romans 4:20–21)

And let us not grow weary while doing good, for in due season we shall reap if we do not lose heart. (Galatians 6:9)

Above all, taking the shield of faith with which you will be able to quench all the fiery darts of the wicked one. (Ephesians 6:16)

Nor give place to the devil. (Ephesians 4:27)

Therefore take up the whole armor of God, that you may be able to withstand in the evil day, and having done all, to stand. (Ephesians 6:13)

That the genuineness of your faith, being much more precious than gold that perishes, though it is tested by fire, may be found to praise, honor, and glory at the revelation of Jesus Christ. (1 Peter 1:7)

Therefore do not cast away your confidence, which has great reward. For you have need of endurance, so that after you have done the will of God, you may receive the promise. (Hebrews 10:35–36)

Let us hold fast the confession of our hope without wavering, for He who promised is faithful. (Hebrews 10:23)

It is important to know that you are born again. God heals those who are believers, and God heals those who are not believers, but it is much easier to receive healing if you know that you are saved. Let's repeat a prayer right now just to be sure that we are:

Father, forgive my sins. I want to be saved. Lord Jesus, come into my heart and make me the kind of person You want me to be. Thank You, Jesus, for coming into my heart and for saving me.

If you prayed that prayer, ask yourself right now, "Where is Jesus?" If your answer is, "In my heart," then you will know that you are saved.

One of the most exciting revelations you can ever have is to discover who you really are in Christ! Once you know that you are saved, it also helps if you will memorize some

Scriptures telling you who you are in Christ. Many people are involved in "churchianity" and "church membership," which are not the equivalent of a personal relationship with Jesus Christ. What is the secret that makes one individual vibrant, with the love of God shining through him, and another one completely defeated? Paul said,

God has sent me to help his Church and to tell his secret plan....He has kept this secret for centuries and generations past, but now at last it has pleased him to tell it to those who love him and live for him, and the riches and glory of his plan are for you Gentiles, too. And this is the secret: Christ in your hearts is your only hope of glory. So everywhere we go we talk about Christ to all who will listen, warning them and teaching them as well as we know how. We want to be able to present each one to God, perfect because of what Christ has done for each of them. This is my work, and I can do it only because Christ's mighty energy is at work within me.
(Colossians 1:25–29 TLB)

"Christ in you, the hope of glory" (verse 27), is the consistent theme throughout Paul's writings. Paul was saying that we cannot live the Christian life on our own. It is only because of Christ living in us that we can!

Charles once saw his spirit outside of his wide-awake, healthy body. It was an exact likeness of his body, but he could clearly see through it. This caused him to see that the Spirit of Jesus merges with our spirits when we are born again. Your part is to find out who you are in Christ!

Christians who are defeated have not yet learned to stand upon the Word and promises of God. Let's see what we have, as born-again believers, according to the Word of God!

In Him we have redemption through His blood, the forgiveness of sins, according to the riches of His grace. (Ephesians 1:7)

Hallelujah, I have redemption and forgiveness of sins!

Therefore, having been justified by faith, we have peace with God through our Lord Jesus Christ. (Romans 5:1)

Glory! I have peace with God!

One of the most important things you can ever have is the ability to lay your head down on a pillow at night and go to sleep quickly because you have peace with God. There are people who would pay literally millions of dollars for peace of mind, and yet they never achieve it.

Consider the following quotation from Billy Rose's *Pitching Horse Shoes*, written in 1948:

In 1923 a very important meeting was held at the Edgewater Beach Hotel in Chicago. In attendance were nine of the world's most successful financiers. Those present were the president of the largest independent steel company, the president of the largest utility company, the president of the largest gas company, the greatest wheat speculator, the president of the New York Stock Exchange, a member of the president's Cabinet, the greatest stock broker, the head of the world's greatest monopoly, and the president of the Bank of International Settlements.

Certainly we must admit that here was gathered a group of the world's most successful men; at least, men who had found the secret of making money. Twenty-five years later, let's see where these men were:

The president of the largest independent steel company, Charles Schwab, died bankrupt and lived on borrowed money for five years before his death. The president of the largest utility company, Samuel Insuff, died a fugitive from justice and penniless in a foreign land. The president of the largest gas company, Howard Hopson, went insane. The greatest wheat speculator, Arthur Cotton, died abroad, insolvent. The president of the New York Stock Exchange, Richard Whitney, was released from Sing Sing Penitentiary. The member of the president's Cabinet, Arthur Fall, was pardoned from prison so he could die at home. The greatest "bear" on Wall Street, Jesse Livermore, died a suicide. The head of the greatest monopoly, Ivan Krueger, died a suicide. The president of the Bank of International Settlements, Leon Fraser, died a suicide. All of these men learned well the art of making a living, but not one learned how to live.

The meeting at the Edgewater Beach Hotel was a youth congress.

Praise God, in Jesus, we have learned how to live!

Even the righteousness of God, through faith in Jesus Christ, to all and on all who believe. For there is no difference. (Romans 3:22)

Every morning when we wake up, Charles and I both say something like, "Good morning, Jesus" or "Jesus, let me love You more," but the second thing we say is, "I have the righteousness of God in me."

Try shouting that some morning from under the covers, and see what it does for you! It can really start your day off right, regardless of how you feel!

One time in Indiana we had just finished a crusade and had gone to bed at midnight. At one o'clock in the morning the Devil took a real poke at me, and I came down with a virus that was probably the most devastating thing that had hit me in years. Hour by hour, I got sicker and sicker, and weaker and weaker. By five o'clock in the morning, I told Charles I thought he and the Amigos (our singing group) would have to go to the next town without me. I said I'd come as soon as I was able.

By the time seven o'clock rolled around, I was so sick, I was almost hoping I would die! But I was too sick for Charles to leave me by myself, so I said, "Don't leave me, honey. Carry me to the bus, and I'll make it somehow!"

I didn't have enough strength to dress, so Charles borrowed a blanket and wrapped it around me. He half-carried me down the stairs and onto the bus. After the most miserable night of my entire life, I can imagine what I looked like! Amigo Chico was driving the bus, and I could tell his heart was breaking because of the way I looked. When I put my foot onto the bottom step of the bus to get on, I looked at him and said, "I have the righteousness of God in me!" I certainly didn't look like it, I certainly didn't feel like it, but I believed what the Word of God says!

After I lay down in one of the bedrooms in the

bus, the Devil continued his field day because the air conditioner stopped working. Without it there is no ventilation on the bus. The temperature seemed to be about 120 degrees inside the bus! The more we drove, the sicker I got, but I kept saying, "I have the righteousness of God in me!" When we arrived at our destination, Charles took me off the bus, put me right to bed, and took the afternoon service alone. Can you guess where I was at seven o'clock that evening? I was standing right with Charles at a miracle service! Hallelujah, I have the righteousness of God in me! God hasn't lost a battle yet!

Say it right now, will you? "I have the righteousness of God in me!" Say it tomorrow morning before you get out of bed, and see what it does to you. God's part has already been done! He put His righteousness in you! Now your part is to believe it!

Christ in you, the hope of glory. (Colossians 1:27)

Put your hand over your heart right now. Do you feel that heartbeat? That's the heartbeat of Jesus Christ living His life in you. When I first realized this, I put my hand over my heart, locked an imaginary door, and threw the key away, saying, "Jesus, I lock You in. Don't You ever get out of there!"

Praise God, I have Christ in me! Say it!

I can do all things through Christ who strengthens me.
(Philippians 4:13)

Do you have a problem over which you can't get victory? Have you tried to quit smoking, only to return to your vomit like a dog does? (See Proverbs 26:11.) Have you tried to quit drinking, only to sneak back again when no one is looking? Have you tried to lose weight, but found yourself back in the kitchen at night gobbling down food over the sink, hoping that if no one caught you, it wouldn't count?

Lots of people think that verse says, "I can do all things *except…*"

Your part is to take hold of that verse for yourself and your need! Say it right now. *"I can do all things through Christ who strengthens me!"*

We have the mind of Christ. (1 Corinthians 2:16)

Did you ever think you weren't as smart as someone else? Did you ever let someone tell you that you were dumb? Don't ever feel that way again! Do you think Jesus was smart? I do.

Therefore, we can't be stupid when we have the mind of Christ!

Say it: "I have the mind of Christ!" Doesn't that make you feel good? Especially if you say it loud!

Do you not know that you are the temple of God and that the Spirit of God dwells in you? (1 Corinthians 3:16)

Praise Jesus, I am the temple of God. I might not look like it to everyone, but God's Word says it, so it's true! I am the temple of God! Glory!

There is therefore now no condemnation to those who are in Christ Jesus, who do not walk according to the flesh, but according to the Spirit. (Romans 8:1)

All my sins have been forgiven. I never have to feel guilty again about anything. Hallelujah! There is no condemnation. A friend of mine who used to drink martinis with me said she felt guilty every time she passed a bar after she was saved. I said, "Not me! Every time I see some drunken woman, I praise God that He saved me from a fate like that." When God forgave me, my part was to accept His forgiveness. I did, and I wouldn't take a drink today if someone offered me fifty million dollars!

What happened to my friend? She didn't stand on the Word of God, that there was now no condemnation, and she went back to drinking!

I have no condemnation because I am in Christ Jesus! Glory to God!

The Spirit Himself bears witness with our spirit that we are children of God. (Romans 8:16)

Praise Jesus, I am a child of God!

For the law of the Spirit of life in Christ Jesus has made me free from the law of sin and death. (Romans 8:2)

I am free from the law of sin and death! Glory!

And if children, then heirs; heirs of God and joint heirs with Christ. (Romans 8:17)

Father, I praise You for giving me the privilege of being
a joint heir with Jesus!

*And we know that all things work together for good to those who love
God, to those who are the called according to His purpose.*
(Romans 8:28)

Sometimes we wonder why certain things happen. In the construction
of our new operations building, the workers fell three months behind
schedule. We needed the space desperately and couldn't understand
why God allowed all the delays to happen. But we kept believing that
"all things work together for good to those who love God." Suddenly we
discovered the reason! Because of expansion that God knew about
all along (but which we didn't know about), if the building
had been completed on schedule, the interior would have
been constructed incorrectly. By God allowing the
delays, we discovered His expansion plans in
time, and made the necessary changes!

Hallelujah, everything works for my good!

If God is for us, who can be against us?
(Romans 8:31)

No one! God and I are a majority!

🌺

We are more than conquerors through Him who loved us.
(Romans 8:37)

🌺

I am a conqueror; therefore, I cannot be defeated!

🌺

For I am persuaded that neither death nor life, nor angels nor principalities nor powers, nor things present nor things to come, nor height nor depth, nor any other created thing, shall be able to separate us from the love of God, which is in Christ Jesus our Lord. (Romans 8:38–39)

🌺

Nothing can separate me from the love of God!

🌺

"The word is near you, in your mouth and in your heart" (that is, the word of faith which we preach).
(Romans 10:8)

🌺

I have the word of faith in my mouth! Praise God!

🌺

For the wages of sin is death, but the gift of God is eternal life in Christ Jesus our Lord.
(Romans 6:23)

🌺

I have eternal life! What more can I ask?

🦋

And my God shall supply all your need according to His riches in glory by Christ Jesus. (Philippians 4:19)

🦋

All my needs shall be met!

🦋

Once you were less than nothing; now you are God's own.
(1 Peter 2:10 TLB)

🦋

I'm somebody, because I belong to God!

🦋

You shall also be a crown of glory in the hand of the LORD, and a royal diadem in the hand of your God. (Isaiah 62:3)

🦋

One night, when I opened my Bible, it fell open to this chapter in Isaiah, and I could hardly believe my eyes to realize that I am a crown of glory and a royal diadem in the hand of the Lord! Glory!

🦋

For God has not given us a spirit of fear, but of power and of love and of a sound mind.
(2 Timothy 1:7)

🦋

Did the Devil ever try to tell you that you were losing your mind, because you couldn't remember as well as you once did? He tried that on me! But I stood on the Word of God and kept telling him that I had power, love, and a sound mind. Would you believe I haven't forgotten a thing since then? (I write everything down!) Fear is one of the most consuming tricks of the Devil these days, and this is a Scripture we ought to say over and over again. I have power, love, and a sound mind, so I don't have to listen to the Devil when he tries to get my mind!

Can you stand any more of the fabulous promises of God? The following Scriptures will give you assurance of the fact that Christ lives within the heart of the believer. God has done His part. He put this truth in His Word. Now your part is to believe it!

Behold, I stand at the door and knock. If anyone hears My voice and opens the door, I will come in to him and dine with him, and he with Me. (Revelation 3:20)

Hallelujah, Jesus is in my heart!

He Himself has said, "I will never leave you nor forsake you." (Hebrews 13:5)

Glory to God, I'll never be alone again!

🦟

If we confess our sins, He is faithful and just to forgive us our sins and to cleanse us from all unrighteousness. (1 John 1:9)

🦟

I am forgiven; I am cleansed!

🦟

So then, those who are in the flesh cannot please God. But you are not in the flesh but in the Spirit, if indeed the Spirit of God dwells in you. Now if anyone does not have the Spirit of Christ, he is not His. And if Christ is in you, the body is dead because of sin, but the Spirit is life because of righteousness. (Romans 8:8–10)

🦟

I have the Spirit of God in me. Hallelujah!

🦟

He who calls you is faithful, who also will do it.
(1 Thessalonians 5:24)

🦟

God will do His part; He said so!

For it is God who works in you both to will and to do for His good pleasure. (Philippians 2:13)

God works in me!

For if when we were enemies we were reconciled to God through the death of His Son, much more, having been reconciled, we shall be saved by His life. (Romans 5:10)

His life saves me!

I have been crucified with Christ; it is no longer I who live, but Christ lives in me; and the life which I now live in the flesh I live by faith in the Son of God, who loved me and gave Himself for me. (Galatians 2:20)

As imperfect as I am, He lives in me!

At that day you will know that I am in My Father, and you in Me, and I in you. He who has My commandments and keeps them, it is he who loves Me. And he who loves Me will be loved by My Father, and I will love him and manifest Myself to him.
(John 14:20–21)

I am in Him! He is in me!

✾

By this we know that we abide in Him, and He in us, because He has given us of His Spirit….Whoever confesses that Jesus is the Son of God, God abides in him, and he in God. And we have known and believed the love that God has for us. God is love, and he who abides in love abides in God, and God in him. (1 John 4:13, 15–16)

✾

I confess that Jesus is the Son of God; therefore, God dwells in me!

✾

Now he who keeps His commandments abides in Him, and He in him. And by this we know that He abides in us, by the Spirit whom He has given us. (1 John 3:24)

✾

I know He abides in me!

✾

"He who believes in Me, as the Scripture has said, out of his heart will flow rivers of living water." But this He spoke concerning the Spirit, whom those believing in Him would receive; for the Holy Spirit was not yet given, because Jesus was not yet glorified. (John 7:38–39)

✾

I believe! I receive!

As a daily prescription, how about saying the following every day:

✸ I have forgiveness of all my sins!

✸ I have peace with God!

✸ I have the righteousness of God in me!

✸ I have Christ in me!

✸ I have power, love, and a sound mind!

✸ I can do all things through Christ!

✸ I have the mind of Christ! I am the temple of God!

✸ I have no condemnation! I am a child of God!

✸ I am free from the law of sin and death!

✸ I am a joint heir with Jesus!

✸ I know that everything works for my good!

✸ I am somebody, because I belong to God!

✸ God and I are a majority!

✸ I am more than a conqueror!

✸ Nothing can separate me from the love of God!

✸ I have the word of faith in my mouth!

✸ I am a crown of glory and a royal diadem!

✸ All my needs shall be met!

✸ I have eternal life!

You have everything when you have Christ!

Hallelujah, I have everything.

Here's some additional good medicine to take daily:

🌸 Jesus is in my heart!

🌸 I'll never be alone again!

🌸 I am forgiven; I am cleansed!

🌸 I have the Spirit of God in me!

🌸 God will do His part!

🌸 God works in me!

🌸 His life saves me!

🌸 He lives in me!

🌸 I am in Him; He is in me!

🌸 God dwells in me!

🌸 I know He abides in me!

🌸 I believe. I receive!

Try these:

🌸 God is always thinking about me!
(1 Peter 5:7 TLB)

🌸 My cup of joy is overflowing! (John 16:24 TLB)

🌸 I am blessed! (Ephesians 1:3)

🌸 My steps are ordered by God. Hallelujah! (Psalm 37:23)

🌸 I have perfect peace. Hallelujah! (Isaiah 26:3)

🌸 I have wisdom. Glory to God! (James 1:5)

🌸 I have joy! (John 15:11)

🌸 My joy is full! (1 John 1:4)

🌸 My strength is renewed! (Isaiah 40:31)

Glory to God! Even as I write these promises, my soul is soaring up into the heavenlies. God has done His wonderful part in giving these promises. Our part is to find them and believe them!*

---

*Originally published in *How Do You Treat My Son Jesus?* by Frances Hunter.

Put Your Faith into Action

Once prayer has been made for you, or once you have read the Scriptures and have read a prayer for yourself, put your faith into action and do something that you could not previously do.

This is one of the things that Charles and I do at every healing meeting. The minute we have laid hands on people, we ask them to do something that they have previously been unable to do, because it is when you put your faith into action that the miracle occurs!

We ask people with a back problem to bend over, and it is when they bend over that the actual healing occurs!

When Jesus prayed for the man who had the withered hand, He said, "Stretch forth your hand." When the man stretched his hand forth, the healing took place. He was not healed until then; it was when he put his faith into action and did something that was impossible for him to do that he actually was healed!

Here are some biblical stories and individual Scriptures that will tell you about people who put their faith into action and what happened as a result of their obedience.

Now Naaman, commander of the army of the king of Syria, was a great and honorable man in the eyes of his master, because by him the LORD had given victory to Syria. He was also a mighty man of valor, but a leper....Then Naaman went with his horses and chariot, and he stood at the door of Elisha's house. And Elisha sent a messenger to him, saying, "Go and wash in the Jordan seven times, and your flesh shall be restored to you, and you shall be clean." But Naaman became furious, and went away and said, "Indeed, I said to myself, 'He will surely come out to me, and stand and call on the name of the LORD his God, and wave his hand over the place, and heal the leprosy.' Are not the Abanah and the Pharpar, the rivers of Damascus, better than all the waters of Israel? Could I not wash in them and be clean?" So he turned and went away in a rage. And his servants came near and spoke to him, and said, "My father, if the prophet had told you to do something great, would you not have done it? How much more then, when he says to you, 'Wash, and be clean'?" So he went down and dipped seven times in the Jordan, according to the saying of the man of God; and his flesh was restored like the flesh of a little child, and he was clean. (2 Kings 5:1, 9–14)

❈

And when he [Jehoshaphat] *had consulted with the people, he appointed those who should sing to the* LORD, *and who should praise the beauty of holiness, as they went out before the army and were saying: "Praise the* LORD, *for His mercy endures forever." Now when they began to sing and to praise, the* LORD *set ambushes against the people of Ammon, Moab, and Mount Seir, who had come against Judah; and they were defeated.*
(2 Chronicles 20:21–22)

❈

And Peter answered Him and said, "Lord, if it is You, command me to come to You on the water." So He said, "Come." And when Peter had come down out of the boat, he walked on the water to go to Jesus. (Matthew 14:28–29)

❈

[Jesus said,] *"I say to you, arise, take up your bed, and go to your house." Immediately he arose, took up the bed, and went out in the presence of them all, so that all were amazed and glorified God, saying, "We never saw anything like this!"* (Mark 2:11–12)

❈

He entered the synagogue again, and a man was there who had a withered hand....And when He had looked around at them with anger, being grieved by the hardness of their hearts, He said to the man, "Stretch out your hand." And he stretched it out, and his hand was restored as whole as the other. (Mark 3:1, 5)

So when He saw them, He said to them, "Go, show yourselves to the priests." And so it was that as they went, they were cleansed. (Luke 17:14)

When he heard that Jesus had come out of Judea into Galilee, he went to Him and implored Him to come down and heal his son, for he was at the point of death. Then Jesus said to him, "Unless you people see signs and wonders, you will by no means believe." The nobleman said to Him, "Sir, come down before my child dies!"...And as [the nobleman] was now going down, his servants met him and told him, saying, "Your son lives!"...So the father knew that it was at the same hour in which Jesus said to him, "Your son lives." And he himself believed, and his whole household. (John 4:47–49, 51, 53)

For we walk by faith, not by sight.
(2 Corinthians 5:7)

Thus also faith by itself, if it does not have works, is dead. But someone will say, "You have faith, and I have works." Show me your faith without your works, and I will show you my faith by my works. You believe that there is one God. You do well. Even the demons believe; and tremble! But do you want to know, O foolish man, that faith without works is dead? Was not Abraham our father justified by works when he offered Isaac his son on the altar? Do you see that faith was working together with his works, and by works faith was made perfect? And the Scripture was fulfilled which says, "Abraham believed God, and it was accounted to him for righteousness." And he was called the friend of God. You see then that a man is justified by works, and not by faith only. Likewise, was not Rahab the harlot also justified by works when she received the messengers and sent them out another way? For as the body without the spirit is dead, so faith without works is dead also.
(James 2:17–26)

Do Something You Couldn't Do

At a recent meeting I had just sat down when I got a case of spiritual goose bumps because a lady tapped me on the shoulder and said, "I'm Anna P."

Your faith will be built as I share this incredible story that happened about twenty years ago in Kalamazoo, Michigan.

This is exactly how Anna shared her story:

Physicians had diagnosed me as a person with five blood diseases. They summed it up to be lupus and gave me only two years to live. They said I would turn into a vegetable. All the things the doctors said would happen to my body did happen, and I ended up in a wheelchair!

My mother in the Lord called me up one night and said that Charles and Frances Hunter would be at First Assembly of God. I was too embarrassed as a woman of God working in the vineyard to go to this meeting, so I was not going. My husband said to me, "Anna, see me pushing you in the wheelchair to the meeting, but see yourself pushing the wheelchair out."

I heard God in that.

They proceeded to get me dressed, and the miracle began.

I was very, very sick. I had pain all over my body, all the time! I was hurting; I heard some things and I didn't hear some things, but I was shaking like a leaf. The same experience happened to me when I was in their presence once before when I received the baptism of the Holy Spirit.

With this manifestation of shaking I knew something was going to happen. As my husband drove me up to the church it was like everyone expected me to come! The ushers came out and wheeled me directly to the front. Honestly, I was so embarrassed because all my family was sitting right in the very front of the church.

Frances got up and began to liven up everything. The joy of the Lord was released all over the place. Frances has a way of getting your faith all "geeked up."

She started teaching on healing and our need for receiving the Word concerning healing.

Suddenly she stopped and said, "Wait a minute; I have to say this now! God said to me that this pretty, young black woman (I did not feel that then) in this wheelchair would hear the Word and God was going to raise her up out of the wheelchair."

By that time I was shaking uncontrollably. I had to pray that the Holy Spirit would hold me to hear the Word. God said she was not to lay hands on me. That was the important part. I would hear the Word spoken, and I would get up out of the wheelchair.

So she began to preach—teaching and preaching—and it got so good that I really started shaking! I struggled because I had to pay attention to what God was going to say! Suddenly she began and then she stopped and said, "Wait, I have to do it now." Then she began to quote Psalm 23.

"The LORD is my shepherd; I shall not want. He makes me to lie down in green pastures; He leads me beside the still waters. He restores my soul; He [guides] me in the paths of righteousness for His name's sake." Then she said, *"Yea, though I walk through the valley of the shadow of death, I will fear no evil."*

I heard this, but I wasn't sure about it, so she said it a second time. I heard, *"I walk…."* I was not walking at all; I was still sitting. But when she said it the third time, *"Yea, though I walk,"* I heard it like this: "I walk."

Then I said to the Lord, "Father, I am not getting out of this chair by myself because I can't do it." He said to me, "I have given you an angel on your right and on your left. Do not be afraid."

When she said, *"Yea, though I walk,"* the angels lifted me up out of the wheelchair, and I did not walk. Instead, He did exceedingly, abundantly above all I could actually think. I RAN! I ran around the whole church! I ran, and I ran, and I ran!

The Devil was still trying to take my legs, but when I was running around the church, Frances pointed at me, and she said, "Wait a minute!" She laid hands on me and said, "The Devil will never again be able to take your legs."

Acting in the name of Jesus, I reminded Satan and my body, "Legs, you don't belong to the Devil!" He can't take my legs.

I ran and ran and ran. It wasn't until after we got out into the parking lot and were getting ready to get into the car that I realized I was pushing the wheelchair! I went back into the church, and I ran again!

Thank God for His Word!

The Bible says, *"He sent His word and healed them, and delivered them from their destructions"* (Psalm 107:20). That's why you must have an ear to hear what God is saying, because when you act on that Word, miracles happen. I mean, it happened when I believed what Frances said.

The thing for me was that I knew I had confidence in the ministry of Charles and Frances Hunter. I knew these were people of God because I [had] received the baptism in their meeting. They've always just been so sweet. I just love this couple.

I knew I heard God through my husband, and throughout the service. But when I heard His Word, and the words in my spirit, *"I walk,"* and I [still] was not walking, I was afraid. I had pain each time I tried to walk.

You know, God knows who we are. He knew that I loved His Word. David said it for me, *"Your word I have hidden in my heart, that I might not sin against You"* (Psalm 119:11). Through all of those years of sickness and disease, I kept my tape recorder under my pillow, listening to the Word of God. Like David, I learned to cry out to God.

The times I was afraid, I said, "I will still trust the Lord." I kept on hearing His Word. I would not let it go. God already knew I was hearing His Word.

He knows who we are. He knows how much we pay attention to His Word. Paying attention to His Word caused me to grow and grow and grow!

What He starts He finishes. Satan does try to come back, but I have to remind him, "I'm not giving up my body to you, Devil."

Different Versions Are Good!

I like to read different versions of the Bible because each one can help in a different way or open one's spiritual eyes to a new dimension.

❧

My son, give attention to my words; incline your ear to my sayings. Do not let them depart from your eyes; keep them in the midst of your heart; for they are life to those who find them, and health to all their flesh.
(Proverbs 4:20–22)

❧

This Scripture needs to be examined and reexamined so that we get everything out of it that is in it!

First of all, it says to give attention to the words of God. Some of the versions say, *"Attend to my words."* What this really means is to give your undivided attention to the words. Open your ears and let yourself hear what the Word of God is saying. Do not under any circumstances let His words depart from your eyes. It is so vital to keep them in the midst of your heart at all times, because then, and only then, you will find life and health.

In Hebrew the word *health* also translates as "medicine." We all need to take the medicine of God.

Did you ever go to a doctor and get a prescription for medicine? Did you ever take the medicine once or twice and decide that was enough and then discover you should have finished the prescription?

The same thing is true of the Word of God. We need to continue His divine medication. The Word of God is life to all who find it and *"health to all their flesh."*

Pay particular attention to the fact that the Scripture doesn't say "part" of their flesh; it says *"all."*

The *Amplified* version reads, *"My son, attend to my words; consent and submit to my sayings. Let them not depart from your sight; keep them in the center of your heart. For they are life to those who find them, healing and health to all their flesh."*

The *Amplified Bible* emphasizes that we need to *"consent and submit"* to the sayings of God. In other words, be willing to do whatever God says. The rest of the verse in the *Amplified Bible* is basically the same as in the *New King James*, but it goes on just a little further to say that not only are God's words life to those who find them, but they are *"healing and health"* to every bit of their flesh—from the top of the head to the tips of the toes! The average person has 125 trillion cells in his body. Each one has the potential to contain the life of God.

The Living Bible reads, *"Listen, son of mine, to what I say. Listen carefully. Keep these thoughts ever in mind; let them penetrate deep within your heart, for they will mean real life for you and radiant health."*

This verse reminds us to keep God's thoughts in our minds at all times. I like this version because it says to let them penetrate deeply—not a shallow penetration—in your heart!

God not only promises you health, but He also promises you *"radiant health,"* which means that your face will glow because of the light of His glory shining from you.

Exodus 15:26 lists four things that are necessary and vital to your healing. If you (1) diligently heed the voice of the Lord your God, (2) do what is right in His sight, (3) give ear to His commandments, and (4) keep all of His statutes, then the following is the result!

I will put none of the diseases on you which I have brought on the Egyptians. For I am the LORD who heals you.
(Exodus 15:26)

First, the beginning of this Scripture is crucial in regard to healing because it indicates that we need to do everything for God diligently—with all of our minds, our hearts, our bodies, and our souls. It doesn't mean that we are to do anything halfheartedly; it means that everything we do is to be done with everything that we have and with excellence. It also means not to just casually listen to God once in a while, but to constantly listen and heed His voice.

Again, the second thing necessary for our healing is that we always do what is right in God's sight. Not just occasionally, but at all times, we must do exactly what is right in His sight!

Third, there are many commandments in the Old Testament; while we operate under grace, the commandments still apply, so we need to give an ear to all of His commandments.

The fourth instruction is to keep all His statutes.

Carefully note that the phrase *"brought on the Egyptians"* in Hebrew means "allowed to come on the Egyptians." This verse would better read, "I will put none of the diseases upon you that I have allowed to come on the Egyptians." The expression *"I am the LORD who heals you"* means that God is our Doctor, our Healer, our Physician.

Who is your doctor? Jesus!

Exodus 23:25–26 repeats that He will take sickness away from you. It says,

So you shall serve the LORD your God, and He will bless your bread and your water. And I will take sickness away from the midst of you. No one shall suffer miscarriage or be barren in your land; I will fulfill the number of your days.

58

Four Powerful Promises

What incredible promises God makes in this passage from Exodus 23! He is going to bless your bread and water so that you don't get sick from your food.

He said, *"I will take sickness* [in the event you are sick] *away from the midst of you."*

There is even a promise for pregnant women. He said, "You will not suffer miscarriage, nor will there be any barren in your land." Many barren women had babies when they took seriously His promise that there would not be any barren in their land. He also said, *"I will fulfill the number of your days."*

And the LORD will take away from you all sickness.
(Deuteronomy 7:15)

The Lord heals all your sicknesses. God doesn't just heal some sicknesses; God's heart wants to heal everything that is wrong with you!

Bless the LORD, *O my soul; and all that is within me, bless His holy name! Bless the* LORD, *O my soul, and forget not all His benefits: who forgives all your iniquities, who heals all your diseases, who redeems your life from destruction, who crowns you with lovingkindness and tender mercies, who satisfies your mouth with good things, so that your youth is renewed like the eagle's.* (Psalm 103:1–5)

This portion of Scripture really impresses me because we have no difficulty believing that God forgives all of our sins, but we seem to have difficulty believing that He also heals all of our diseases. I firmly believe that if we had understood a lot more about God's Word when we were saved, we would all have been healed instantly at the time of our salvation. This verse is full of promises; we need to accept not only the forgiveness of our sins, but also the healing of any and all physical problems that we may have in our bodies.

I also like the verse in the *Amplified* version. It says,

Bless (affectionately, gratefully praise) the Lord, O my soul; and all that is [deepest] within me, bless His holy name! Bless (affectionately, gratefully praise) the Lord, O my soul, and forget not [one of] all His benefits—who forgives [every one of] all your iniquities, who heals [each one of] all your diseases. (Psalm 103:1–3)

You see, God isn't interested in healing just one little portion of you. God wants to heal every part of you.

Isaiah 53:4–5 gives us some strong words:

Surely He has borne our griefs [in Hebrew that means sickness] *and carried our sorrows* [in Hebrew that means pains]; *yet we esteemed Him stricken, smitten by God, and afflicted. But He was wounded for our transgressions, He was bruised for our iniquities; the chastisement for our peace was upon Him, and by His stripes we are healed.*

Surely He has borne our griefs (sicknesses, weaknesses, and distresses) and carried our sorrows and pains [of punishment], yet we [ignorantly] considered Him stricken, smitten, and afflicted by God [as if with leprosy]. But He was wounded for our transgressions, He was bruised for our guilt and iniquities; the chastisement [needful to obtain] peace and well-being for us was upon Him, and with the stripes [that wounded] Him we are healed and made whole. (Isaiah 53:4–5 AMP)

They put thirty-nine stripes on the back of Jesus when they scourged Him, and in those stripes was every disease that you have. Deeply imbedded in those stripes were your arthritis, your multiple sclerosis, your diabetes, your cancer, or whatever you have! Jesus took it in one of those horrible, bloody stripes on His back. Take hold of the Word of God right now and say, "Jesus, You took my disease for me. I don't need to take it because by Your stripes I was healed. The healing has already been accomplished. Instead of receiving sickness and disease, I receive healing."

62

Here are some excellent promises. I encourage you not only to learn the promises of God, but also to begin to state in your own words what these promises mean to you and do for you!

Let your heart retain my words; keep my commands, and live. (Proverbs 4:4)

Say something like, "Thank You, Father; I'm going to live because I am retaining Your words."

The curse of the LORD is on the house of the wicked, but He blesses the home of the just. (Proverbs 3:33)

"Thank you, Lord, that my house is not wicked, but is a just house; therefore, sickness cannot stay in my body."

Now therefore, listen to me, my children, for blessed are those who keep my ways....For whoever finds me finds life, and obtains favor from the LORD. (Proverbs 8:32, 35)

"Praise the Lord, not only do I have health, but I also have favor with God!" And when the favor of God is on you, no evil can harm you.

🐝

The labor of the righteous leads to life, the wages of the wicked to sin. (Proverbs 10:16)

🐝

"Praise the Lord, my work shall bring me life." Every time you see the word *life* in the Word of God, it means "health," so your work will bring you health.

🐝

The fear of the LORD prolongs days, but the years of the wicked will be shortened. (Proverbs 10:27)

🐝

"Hallelujah; I am going to live a long life."

🐝

The way of the LORD is strength for the upright, but destruction will come to the workers of iniquity. (Proverbs 10:29)

🐝

"Praise God, praise God, praise God! Because I'm walking with the Lord, I have strength!" Aren't you glad that you have strength because you are walking with the Lord? Aren't you delighted that weakness can't come into your life?

Watch Your Mouth

Do you know that your mouth can be a snare to your soul, too? You can get up in the morning and say, "Oh, I feel sick. I feel terrible. My arthritis hurts; everything hurts." Do you know what is going to happen? Everything is going to hurt just exactly like you said! Remember this:

There is one who speaks like the piercings of a sword, but the tongue of the wise promotes health. (Proverbs 12:18)

The *Amplified Bible*'s translation of this verse has something very good to show us, also. Remember, you can really be trapped by what you say! Recently I had the most miserable sore throat I have ever had in my entire life! I was scheduled to record audio tapes, and every time I started to record, the Devil came in and really tried to attack my throat. Instead of accepting the attack, I sat at the breakfast table and screamed at the top of my lungs, "By His stripes I am healed! Devil, you can't have my throat any more." I want you to know that my throat cleared up instantly and hasn't been sore since!

Here's how the verse reads in the *Amplified* version:

There are those who speak rashly, like the piercing of a sword, but the tongue of the wise brings healing. (Proverbs 12:18)

There's good advice contained in this version about not speaking rashly! Remember, your own tongue can bring healing to you instead of destruction!

What does a wise man do? He quotes the Word of God. Try saying it aloud right now.

Bless the LORD, O my soul, and forget not all His benefits: who forgives all your iniquities, who heals all your diseases.
(Psalm 103:2–3)

"Thank You, Lord, that my diseases are healed. I am confessing healing with my mouth right now because *"the tongue of the wise brings healing"* (Proverbs 12:18 AMP).

A wholesome tongue is a tree of life, but perverseness in it breaks the spirit. (Proverbs 15:4)

"My tongue speaks the Word of God and is wholesome. Negativity shall never be a part of my vocabulary."

A merry heart does good, like medicine, but a broken spirit dries the bones. (Proverbs 17:22)

It is time to have joy in your life because *"a merry heart does good, like medicine."* When your heart is happy, it is the same as taking a good dose of the medicine of God!

The *Amplified* version of Proverbs 17:22 states an additional "God-thought": *"A happy heart is good medicine and a cheerful mind works healing, but a broken spirit dries up the bones."*

This verse brings the attitude of your mind into healing. Isn't it tremendous to know that a cheerful mind is going to work healing in your body?

"My mind is going to be cheerful, and I have a happy heart, so I'm taking good medicine! Hallelujah, Lord, I'm going to praise You; I'm going to love You! I'm going to worship You, and my bones are never going to be dry."

Death and life are in the power of the tongue, and those who love it will eat its fruit. (Proverbs 18:21)

"Hallelujah, I have life in my tongue! I don't speak death; I speak life! Lord, from now on, I'm going to be watching my words very carefully so I can eat lots of delicious fruit!"

The fear of the LORD leads to life, and he who has it will abide in satisfaction; he will not be visited with evil. (Proverbs 19:23)

"Praise God that, because I reverence the Lord, I have health and will not be visited by evil. Glory!"

By humility and the fear of the LORD are riches and honor and life. (Proverbs 22:4)

You are not only going to be healthy, but you're also going to have riches and honor besides by humility and fear of the Lord. Hallelujah! These are all yours! Confess and believe that Scripture right now!

One of my favorite Scriptures on healing is one that a lot of people don't realize concerns healing. Many people think it concerns

68

prosperity, and it does. However, it actually concerns both, because it says,

Blessed is the man who walks not in the counsel of the ungodly, nor stands in the path of sinners, nor sits in the seat of the scornful; but his delight is in the law of the LORD [and that's the Word of God], and in His law he meditates day and night. He shall be like a tree planted by the rivers of water, that brings forth its fruit in its season, whose leaf also shall not wither. (Psalm 1:1–3)

What makes a leaf wither and die? When it is not healthy and when it is not getting nourishment from the vine, then it withers and dies. We do not walk in the counsel of the ungodly; we do not stand in the path of sinners, nor do we sit in the seat of the scornful; but our [that's yours and mine] delight is in the law of the Lord, and in His law we meditate day and night. Therefore, we are going to be like trees planted by the rivers of water that bring forth fruit in season. I want you to say this with me right now: "My leaf shall not wither. My leaf shall not wither, and whatever I do shall prosper!"

Every time you read, "His leaf will not wither," I want you to say, "I will not be sick." Why? "Because I'm fulfilling the conditions that God laid down!"

❋

The Lord will give strength to His people; the Lord will bless His people with peace. (Psalm 29:11)

❋

Glory to God for His strength! The Lord will give strength.

"Thank You, Lord, for strength in my body right now!" Expect a surge of resurrection power to come into your body! And it says, *"The Lord will bless His people with peace."*

"Thank You, Lord, because You give peace even in the most troubled times."

❋

O Lord my God, I cried out to You, and You healed me. (Psalm 30:2)

❋

That is the Scripture that spoke to me when I was healed of diabetes. If you have ever cried out to God for healing, say the following right now!

Thank You, Lord. Thank You, Lord, because You have healed me. I praise You, Lord, because You healed me. I worship You, Lord, because You healed me. Oh, thank You, Lord, for the promises of God. Thank You, Lord, for the promises of God.

You can never thank Him enough!

Look at this:

🦋

For the LORD *God is a sun and shield; the* LORD *will give grace and glory; no good thing will He withhold from those who walk uprightly.* (Psalm 84:11)

🦋

Is your health a good thing? Is your healing a good thing? Yes, it is! One of the most important things to you right now is to be healed. Because the Bible says, *"No good thing will He withhold from those who walk uprightly,"* nothing is going to be withheld from you, including your healing! What a wonderful promise of God!

🦋

He sent His word and healed them. (Psalm 107:20)

🦋

The Word of God can heal you! When the Word of God becomes quickened in your heart, the Word of God can heal you! The best way to really make the Word of God quicken in your heart is to say Scriptures out loud! If you read this book over and over until you have memorized many of the Scriptures that are included within it, you can be healed by the time you have finished several readings. It is when you constantly keep putting the words of God back into your mind, and when you speak those words, that things begin to happen! When you read the Word, you see it with your eyes; but when you speak it, you see it with your eyes, you speak it with your mouth, and you hear it with your ears!

To help you, I would like to suggest that you get your tape recorder and record the healing Scriptures with your own voice and then listen to your own voice as you look at the Word of God.

There can be such a tremendous improvement in your health so fast that it is going to be difficult for you to believe it. Praise God for His Word right now!

He heals the brokenhearted and binds up their wounds.
(Psalm 147:3)

Not only does God want to heal your physical body, but He also wants to heal your heart, because a "sick" heart can bring sickness!

And the prayer of faith will save the sick, and the Lord will raise him up. (James 5:15)

"Lord, right now I pray this prayer of faith. Father, in the name of Jesus, I stand upon the Word of God because You said You sent Your Word and healed them (Psalm 107:20). I ask You to heal every part of my body and raise me up from my bed of affliction! I thank You for it, and I praise Your holy name."

Who Himself bore our sins in His own body on the tree, that we, having died to sins, might live for righteousness; by whose stripes you were healed. (1 Peter 2:24)

Hallelujah, it's done! It's finished! It's completed! I was healed.

What did Jesus do? Jesus went around all of Galilee teaching in the synagogues, preaching the Gospel of the kingdom, and healing all manner of sickness and all manner of disease among the people. Many times we need a little teaching before we can receive a healing from the Word of God.

I will take sickness away from the midst of you. (Exodus 23:25)

Thank You, Lord, for this promise. Thank You that You are removing sickness from me as far as the east is from the west, never to return again.

Then He called His twelve disciples together and gave them power and authority over all demons, and to cure diseases. (Luke 9:1)

Jesus gave power to His disciples, and anyone who is a follower of Jesus is still a disciple, so you have the power to cure diseases! Then He sent them to preach the kingdom of God and to heal the sick.

Thank You, Jesus, for that power! Thank You that I can let one of the elders of my church lay hands on me and I can receive healing because Jesus gave us authority to heal the sick!

I shall not die, but live, and declare the works of the LORD. (Psalm 118:17)

If you have a "fatal" disease, this is one of the

most beautiful verses in the Bible, and the verse I would stand on!

Say it again and again: *"I shall not die, but live, and declare the works of the Lord."* Repeat this Scripture aloud several times.

Behold, I am the Lord, the God of all flesh. Is there anything too hard for Me? (Jeremiah 32:27)

Praise God, nothing is too hard for Him! It doesn't make any difference what your problem is; there is nothing too hard for God. Continue agreeing with God: "Thank You, Lord; there is nothing too hard for You. My cancer is not too hard, my diabetes is not too hard, my crippled foot is not too hard for You. Nothing is too hard for You!"

Every day of my life from now on I will sing my songs of praise in the Temple. (Isaiah 38:20 TLB)

Think of it! The Lord healed me! Isn't it exciting to know that you have been healed by God? God wants to heal you. God doesn't want anybody to be sick!

Beloved, I pray that you may prosper in all things and be in health, just as your soul prospers. (3 John 2)

Beloved, I want you to study these particular verses from the Word of God. Read these healing Scriptures over and over again until you are so completely saturated with the Word of God that it is just running all over and out of you. Allow His Word to flow out of your mouth, out of your eyes, out of your ears. Then be sure to thank Him; be sure to praise Him for the very fact that He has healed you. Then you can truthfully get up and say, "The Lord healed me!" Think of it! Hallelujah!

God tells us to shout from the housetops the things that He does for us. The minute you know you are healed, just stand up and shout it to the world.

Conditions for Staying Healed

There are conditions to many of God's promises. Thus, it is just as necessary to maintain your healing as it is to get your healing. The following portion of Isaiah 58 is very interesting because it tells you how to remain healthy.

No, the kind of fast I want is that you stop oppressing those who work for you and treat them fairly and give them what they earn. I want you to share your food with the hungry and bring right into your own homes those who are helpless, poor, and destitute. Clothe those who are cold, and don't hide from relatives who need your help. If you do these things, God will shed his own glorious light upon you. He will heal you; your godliness will lead you forward, goodness will be a shield before you, and the glory of the Lord will protect you from behind. Then, when you call, the Lord will answer. "Yes, I am here," he will quickly reply. [In other words, you are going to get your prayers answered.] *All you need to do is to stop oppressing the weak and stop making false accusations and spreading vicious rumors! Feed the hungry! Help those in trouble! Then your light will shine out from the darkness, and the darkness around you shall be as bright as day. And the Lord will guide you continually, and satisfy you with all good things, and keep you healthy too; and you will be like a well-watered garden, like an ever-flowing spring.*
(Isaiah 58:6–11 TLB)

Isn't that a fantastic promise of God? Remember, different versions give you different perspectives on God's Word. Let's read the *New King James Version:*

🌿

Is this not the fast that I have chosen: to loose the bonds of wickedness, to undo the heavy burdens, to let the oppressed go free, and that you break every yoke? Is it not to share your bread with the hungry, and that you bring to your house the poor who are cast out; when you see the naked, that you cover him, and not hide yourself from your own flesh? Then your light shall break forth like the morning, your healing shall spring forth speedily, and your righteousness shall go before you; the glory of the Lord *shall be your rear guard.* [Nothing demonic in nature can sneak up on you!] *Then you shall call, and the* Lord *will answer; you shall cry, and He will say, "Here I am." If you take away the yoke from your midst, the pointing of the finger, and speaking wickedness, if you extend your soul to the hungry and satisfy the afflicted soul, then your light shall dawn in the darkness, and your darkness shall be as the noonday. The* Lord *will guide you continually, and satisfy your soul in drought, and strengthen your bones; you shall be like a watered garden, and like a spring of water, whose waters do not fail.*

🌿

Hallelujah! Your healing is going to *"spring forth speedily"*! You are going to be like the living water when you do the things described in this passage.

🦟

Blessings on all who reverence and trust the Lord—on all who obey him! Their reward shall be prosperity and happiness. Your wife shall be contented in your home. And look at all those children! There they sit around the dinner table as vigorous and healthy as young olive trees. That is God's reward to those who reverence and trust him. May the Lord continually bless you with heaven's blessings as well as with human joys. May you live to enjoy your grandchildren! And may God bless Israel! (Psalm 128 TLB)

🦟

Isn't it beautiful that not only you can be healthy, but your family can be healthy as well?

Let's look at this passage in the *New King James Version:*

*Blessed is every one who fears the LORD, who walks in His ways.
When you eat the labor of your hands, you shall be happy, and it shall
be well with you. Your wife shall be like a fruitful vine in the very heart
of your house, your children like olive plants all around your table. Behold,
thus shall the man be blessed who fears the LORD. The LORD bless you out
of Zion, and may you see the good of Jerusalem all the days of your life. Yes,
may you see your children's children. Peace be upon Israel!*

I have to stop here and tell you something that I think might be of
tremendous interest to you. About forty years ago, doctors gave
me two months to live. They said that there was absolutely no
hope whatsoever. The bad report was that I had two diseases,
both of which are fatal! One was called Addison's Disease,
and the other one was called Myxdema. I didn't even
look like a human being. Every day, by the time
nightfall came, my skin would turn so dark
that it was almost impossible to recognize me.
It was a horrible gray color. There were many
times when I would fall sound asleep sitting
in a chair and sometimes sleep for three days
without anyone ever being able to wake me
up. This was years before I became

a Christian, but I remember crying out to God one night and saying, "Oh, God! Let me live long enough to raise my children."

God answered my prayer, and, in His love, mercy, and grace, He healed me the day I made Jesus the Lord of my life! More than thirty-five years later, I am probably one of the healthiest persons you could know. There is no sign of Myxdema. There is no sign of Addison's Disease!

The thing that really caught me about Psalm 128 was where it said that I could even enjoy my grandchildren! That just really gets me so excited because it said that I was going to live not only to raise my children, but to raise my grandchildren as well!

I praise the Lord for my eight grandchildren. *"Yes, may you see your children's children."* I praise the Lord that my son has four children, and that my daughter also has four. God has let me live to see all of them, and I'm expecting to live to see all of them raised unless Jesus Christ comes back, and then we'll all be caught up at the same time. Hallelujah!

Faith Is Always Required

I have to be honest with you. Faith is also involved in healing. I do not know the exact amount of faith you need to be healed because sometimes I have ministered to people who didn't seem to have any faith at all, and yet they were healed!

Other times I've ministered to people whom I thought had great faith, and apparently they weren't healed.

The Word of God has a lot to say about praying with faith and believing.

You might be saying, "I don't have as much faith as you do." Yes, you do! The first chapter of 2 Peter tells us we all have the same measure of faith from God. (See verse 1.) We don't have to wish that we had the same kind of faith as another person, because we already have it! But it is what we add to our faith that makes it seem greater. I have a lot more faith today than the day I was saved. Do you know why? Because I have stepped out in that faith. I have let God do what

He wanted to do. And when I see God perform what He says He is going to perform, then my faith really stretches out! We must add to our faith. Let me give you a very good example of this.

God has given us a tremendous ministry in back healings. Many times a back problem is revealed in either a short arm or a short leg. The first time I prayed when someone came to me with a short arm—I have to be honest with you—I prayed and I don't even know if I believed it or not! I think probably more than anything else I was standing there hoping that God would do something. And God did it! The arm grew out. What do you think happened to my faith? My faith really grew because I prayed, and God did it. The little measure of faith that God gave me when I was saved grew because I added to it; I gave God the opportunity to prove that His Word is actually true.

Today Charles and I have 100-percent faith for back problems! There isn't a back problem in the world that Charles and I don't pray for and believe with our minds, our hearts, our bodies, and our souls that God is going to heal.

Do you want more and more of God's kindness and peace? Then learn to know him better and better. For as you know him better, he will give you, through his great power, everything you need for living a truly good life: he even shares his own glory and his own goodness with us! And by that same mighty power he has given us all the other rich and wonderful blessings he promised; for instance, the promise to save us from the lust and rottenness all around us, and to give us his own character. But to obtain these gifts, you need more than faith....[Now, this is how you do it.] *You must learn to know God better and discover what he wants you to do.* (2 Peter 1:2–5 TLB)

God gives to each one of us exactly the same measure of faith!

We are told to get into the Word of God because there is absolutely nothing that will give you more faith, or will build your faith more, than when you read the Bible in a personal way. It says, *"You must learn to know God better and discover what he wants you to do."* You can't know what God wants you to do unless you get into His Word!

Next, learn to put aside your own desires. The *New King James Version* says to add knowledge, self-control, perseverance, and then godliness to your faith. To godliness you should add brotherly kindness, and to brotherly kindness love (2 Peter 1:5–7). There are many times when we need to have our faith layered. Sometimes we put down one little tiny layer of faith, and then we wonder why we don't have more. We need to put down a second layer, a third, a fourth, a fifth, and keep building our faith until it is at a point when it will literally explode!

Many times we need a point of contact or a touching point!

A number of years ago a lady was very sick and was not expected to live. She was in bed and sent word to me: "If Frances could just come to my house, and I could just touch the hem of her garment, I know I would be healed."

Beloved, I want you to know there is no power in the hem of any garment I own—not a single, solitary power! But that was a touching point for this certain woman. So, I went over and found her lying on the floor in the living room on just a mattress—no bed frame, no box springs! When I walked over and started to kneel down, she touched the hem of my dress. That was a touching point for her, and her faith instantly healed her!

That was thirty years ago, and she is enjoying beautiful

and radiant health today. Why? Because her faith got her to the point where she said, "If I could just touch the hem of Frances' garment, I would be healed. And I know it." Her faith reached a point—her faith reached a condition! She had the faith of God to begin with. It was just a tiny measure, but she kept hearing about the healings that had been happening in my ministry. That's why she said she knew that God would heal her.

God declares Himself as the One who heals.

❦

For I am the LORD who heals you. (Exodus 15:26)

❦

I wound and I heal. (Deuteronomy 32:39)

❦

I have seen your tears; surely I will heal you.
(2 Kings 20:5)

❦

"I have seen his ways, and will heal him; I will also lead him, and restore comforts to him and to his mourners. I create the fruit of the lips: Peace, peace to him who is far off and to him who is near," says the LORD, "and I will heal him." (Isaiah 57:18–19)

❦

Pleasant words are as a honeycomb, sweet to the mind and healing to the body. (Proverbs 16:24 AMP)

Many times people who are sick don't really feel like being very nice to you! But we need to remember that if we will keep our words as sweet and pleasant as honeycomb, they will also be healing to the body.

The Living Bible reads, *"Kind words are like honey—enjoyable and healthful."* We should always remember that, whenever we feel like saying something unkind, pleasant words are healing to the body. Our "tune" will change in a hurry.

"A gentle tongue [with its healing power] is a tree of life, but willful contrariness in it breaks down the spirit" (Proverbs 15:4 AMP). A gentle tongue has healing power; therefore, you are a tree of life.

Gentle words cause life and health; griping brings discouragement. (TLB)

Always make sure that your words are gentle. Make sure they are pleasant. Make sure that you have a merry

heart because all of these things add up to give you
good health.

※

*The light in the eyes [of him whose heart is joyful] rejoices the hearts of
others, and good news nourishes the bones.* (Proverbs 15:30 AMP)

※

Good reports give happiness and health. (TLB)

※

If you will speak the Word of God, and refuse to speak in condemnation,
but speak it in joy and speak the promises, you will even speak healing
to others and nourish your own bones. No arthritis! Hallelujah!

※

*The light of the eyes rejoices the heart, and a good report makes the
bones healthy.* (NKJV)

※

*O Lord my God, I pleaded with you, and you gave me my
health again. You brought me back from the brink of
the grave, from death itself, and here I am alive!*
(Psalm 30:2–3 TLB)

※

Glory to God! Isn't it beautiful to know that you
can cry unto God and He will give you your health
again? I always put my name in there and say,
"Lord, I pleaded with You, and You gave
me my health again."

Oh, thank You, Lord; I am so grateful. I love You, I praise You, and I worship You. Thank You, Father, for the fact that You heal bodies even in the twenty-first century. We give You the praise and the glory, Father, because we know that You do it all.

Then Daniel praised the God of heaven, saying, "Blessed be the name of God forever and ever, for he alone has all wisdom and all power. World events are under his control. He removes kings and sets others on their thrones. He gives wise men their wisdom and scholars their intelligence. He reveals profound mysteries beyond man's understanding. He knows all hidden things, for he is light, and darkness is no obstacle to him. I thank and praise you, O God of my fathers, for you have given me wisdom and glowing health." (Daniel 2:19–23 TLB)

Notice that all these people in the Bible praised God, and that's what we need to do. Praise God, praise God, praise God!

Isn't it wonderful to know that God will give you *"glowing health"*? "God, I take that glowing health right now for my very own." Do you know something else? God promises end-time health, and we are definitely in the end times.

These next two verses talk about the end times and tell you what kind of health God's children are going to have.

🌿

The Lord their God will save his people in that day, as a Shepherd caring for his sheep. They shall shine in his land as glittering jewels in a crown. How wonderful and beautiful all shall be! The abundance of grain and grapes will make the young men and girls flourish; they will be radiant with health and happiness. (Zechariah 9:16–17 TLB)

🌿

We can be radiant with health and happiness.

🌿

"Rejoice with Jerusalem; be glad with her, all you who love her, you who mourned for her. Delight in Jerusalem; drink deep of her glory even as an infant at a mother's generous breasts. Prosperity shall overflow Jerusalem like a river," says the Lord, "for I will send it; the riches of the Gentiles will flow to her. Her children shall be nursed at her breasts, carried on her hips and dandled on her knees. I will comfort you there as a little one is comforted by its mother. When you see Jerusalem, your heart will rejoice; vigorous health will be yours." (Isaiah 66:10–14 TLB)

🌿

And when you see Jerusalem, what is that?
It is the kingdom of God!

It is wonderful to know that vigorous health is yours and mine, because that means I can continue running all over the United States and all over the world. Charles and I are going to have vigorous and glowing health.

"For I will restore health to you and heal you of your wounds," says the LORD. (Jeremiah 30:17)

God promises to restore health unto you and heal you of your wounds!

My son, attend to my words; consent and submit to my sayings. Let them not depart from your sight; keep them in the center of your heart. For they are life to those who find them, healing and health to all their flesh. Keep and guard your heart with all vigilance and above all that you guard, for out of it flow the springs of life. (Proverbs 4:20–23 AMP)

Out of it shall flow springs of life—not death, but life!

Be not wise in your own eyes; reverently fear and worship the Lord and turn [entirely] away from evil. (Proverbs 3:7 AMP)

Do this and see what the promise is. It says, *"It shall be health to your nerves and sinews, and marrow and moistening to your bones"* (verse 8 AMP). What happens to your bones when they get dry? They get brittle, they break, and you die. When that life-flowing substance is taken out of the marrow of your bones, you are not going to be here much longer.

✻

Listen, son of mine, to what I say. Listen carefully. Keep these thoughts ever in mind; let them penetrate deep within your heart, for they will mean real life for you and radiant health. (Proverbs 4:20–22 TLB)

✻

If you want favor with both God and man, and a reputation for good judgment and common sense, then trust the Lord completely; don't ever trust yourself. In everything you do, put God first, and he will direct you and crown your efforts with success. Don't be conceited, sure of your own wisdom. Instead, trust and reverence the Lord, and turn your back on evil; when you do that, then you will be given renewed health and vitality. (Proverbs 3:4–8 TLB)

✻

Did you read that? When you trust and reverence the Lord and you turn your back on evil, you are going to be given renewed health and vitality. Glory to God! Doesn't that really make you excited? All I know is that it really excites me because I know I'm going to live in health and vitality all the days of my life.

Evil spelled backwards is *live!*

I recently reread the story about Hezekiah in Isaiah 38. I want you to pay close attention to this, because so many of the conditions of God are met when you do certain things. If you will do what the Word of God says, then God is going to do His part. This was just before Hezekiah became deathly ill and Isaiah went to visit him and gave him the message from the Lord. As a matter of fact, Isaiah told him to get his affairs straightened out because he was going to die. But then Hezekiah cried out to the Lord. This is what he said:

All night I moaned; it was like being torn apart by lions. Delirious, I chattered like a swallow and mourned like a dove; my eyes grew weary of looking up for help. "O God," I cried, "I am in trouble—help me." But what can I say? For he himself has sent this sickness. All my sleep has fled because of my soul's bitterness.
(Isaiah 38:13–15 TLB)

And beloved, bitterness can really cause illnesses.

O Lord, your discipline is good and leads to life and health. Oh, heal me and make me live! (Isaiah 38:16 TLB)

Did you hear what he said? God's discipline is good because it leads to life and health. When you obey the Word of God, you are going to be healthy.

Yes, now I see it all—it was good for me to undergo this bitterness, for you have lovingly delivered me from death; you have forgiven all my sins. For dead men cannot praise you. They cannot be filled with hope and joy. The living, only the living, can praise you as I do today. One generation makes known your faithfulness to the next. Think of it! The Lord healed me! Every day of my life from now on I will sing my songs of praise in the Temple, accompanied by the orchestra.
(Isaiah 38:17–20 TLB)

Try to grasp what Hezekiah meant when he said *"Think of it"* in that beautiful Scripture. He was so grateful for his healing that he said he would sing songs of praise every day of his life. That is exactly what God wants all of us to do. When we receive a healing, let's tell the world about it, and let's continue to thank Him and praise Him every single day.

As I have often said, I have more new parts than I have original parts because of God's love, mercy, and grace. I thank Him every day of my life for the healing He has put in my body. Right now, say, "Lord, You've healed me, and I thank You for it. I give You all the praise and glory, and I will do this every day of life! I love You, I praise You, I worship You, and I thank You for Your compassion in healing me."

Are you willing to spend the rest of your life praising God and singing songs of praise to Him because of what He has done for you? I think it's a wonderful witness when the Lord heals us and we go out and tell everybody what God has done in our lives.

Jesus heals all kinds of sicknesses. It doesn't make any difference what kind of healing you need. Believe that Jesus is going to do it, and His promise is that He will do it.

Let's go back to this beautiful verse:

Blessed is the man who walks not in the counsel of the ungodly, nor stands in the path of sinners, nor sits in the seat of the scornful; but his delight is in the law of the LORD, and in His law he meditates day and night. He shall be like a tree planted by the rivers of water, that brings forth its fruit in its season, whose leaf also shall not wither; and whatever he does shall prosper. (Psalm 1:1–3)

Beloved, get into the Word of God; meditate on it day and night. Read it, and reread it. Read His promises over and over again. Don't just read them in one version; read every Bible translation that you have in your house. Read them until they are quickened in your heart. Then something will happen.

Beloved, your promise of health is found in the above verses. You are not going to be sick. You are not going to wither, and you are not going to fall off the vine. Whatever you do will prosper.

❧

Oh, the joys of those who do not follow evil men's advice, who do not hang around with sinners, scoffing at the things of God. But they delight in doing everything God wants them to, and day and night are always meditating on his laws and thinking about ways to follow him more closely. (Psalm 1:1–2 TLB)

❧

Father, in the name of Jesus, I speak the word of healing to everyone who reads this and who needs Your touch. In the middle of their reading this book I ask that You touch them, Jesus. We thank You and praise You. Amen.

More Medicine!

"Faith comes by hearing, and hearing by the word of God" (Romans 10:17). Oftentimes you will hear speakers say, "Faith comes by hearing and hearing and hearing and hearing and hearing and hearing and hearing the Word of God." One way to healing is by obeying God and continually confessing Scriptures.

You can never listen to the Word of God too much! You can never read the Word of God too much! You can never absorb the Word of God too much, because healing resides in the Word of God!

🦋

But to you who fear My name The Sun of Righteousness shall arise with healing in His wings; and you shall go out and grow fat like stall-fed calves. (Malachi 4:2)

🦋

But for you who fear my name, the Sun of Righteousness will rise with healing in His wings. And you will go free, leaping with joy like calves let out to pasture. (TLB)

🦋

That's what I want to do! Go leaping with joy!

We need to trust the Word of God and believe what God says. We need to believe with everything in us that the Sun of Righteousness will rise with healing in His wings!

In the Old Testament the Sun of Righteousness means Jesus. In Jesus there is healing for whatever problem you have in your life. God doesn't want you to be sick. Believe that with your heart and with your soul!

Let's go to some of the Scriptures in the New Testament that I believe will firmly convince you of the fact that God does not want you to be sick. In those stripes on the back of Jesus, He took every disease that you have. It doesn't make any difference at all whether it's cancer, epilepsy, diabetes, arthritis, a brain tumor, or any other disease; it is not God's will for you to be sick.

Jesus went about all Galilee, teaching in their synagogues, preaching the gospel of the kingdom, and healing all kinds of sickness and all kinds of disease among the people. Then His fame went throughout all Syria; and they brought to Him all sick people who were afflicted with various diseases and torments, and those who were demon-possessed, epileptics, and paralytics; and He healed them. (Matthew 4:23–24)

The Word of God says, *"And He healed them."*

That's exactly why it is so important to believe that God intends for us to be healed. I want you to notice something else. Notice that before it mentions the fact that He went around healing them all, it says that He went everywhere preaching the good news about the kingdom of heaven.

I believe there are many times when people do not get healed because they do not understand the Word of God. They will try quoting one verse of Scripture, and when they are not healed, they can't understand why it didn't work!

We need a good understanding of the Word of God in order to know what God has to say. There is no substitute for knowing what Jesus did in the area of healing.

When God put us in the miracle ministry, the eighth chapter of Matthew was one of the chapters that Charles and I studied over and over again. Jesus didn't always heal the same way. When you are out in a ministry where people come to you for healing, you need to know to the best of your ability how Jesus healed.

When He had come down from the mountain, great multitudes followed Him. And behold, a leper came and worshiped Him, saying, "Lord, if You are willing, You can make me clean." Then Jesus put out His hand and touched him, saying, "I am willing; be cleansed." Immediately his leprosy was cleansed. And Jesus said to him, "See that you tell no one; but go your way, show yourself to the priest, and offer the gift that Moses commanded, as a testimony to them." (Matthew 8:1–4)

The leper came to Jesus. Notice that Jesus did not go to the leper; the leper came to Jesus! He said, *"Lord, if You are willing, You can make me clean."* Jesus said the words that I believe He is saying to you today. He said, *"I am willing; be cleansed."* If you are saying to Him, "Jesus, if You are willing, You can heal me," then Jesus is saying to you exactly as He said to the leper, "I am willing; be healed."

The first thing He said to the leper was, "Go back to the doctor [that was the priest], show yourself to him, and let him be the one who says you are healed." Jesus knew all along that the man was healed. The man didn't have to go back to the priest and have it verified that he was healed. People today say, "If I go back and have the doctor examine me, that doesn't show faith." Yes, it does.

People do not always believe you, but they will believe the doctor!

When I had a problem with my heart and God gave me a brand new heart, I went right back to the same doctor who had previously examined me. I went back to the same hospital where they had taken the X-rays the first time, which had showed the enlarged heart with a hole in it. I went right back to the same place, and there, standing side by side, were two X-rays. One showed an enlarged heart. The other one showed a perfectly normal heart.

I went right back to the "priest" and showed myself. In other words, I went right back to the doctor and had the doctor perform the same tests he had performed the first time. This action confirmed that God had healed me because nothing else could have done it.

Jesus wants you to be healed. He doesn't want you to be sick. When you say to Him, "If You are willing, You can make me whole," Jesus is going to say, "I am willing; be made whole."

Now when Jesus had entered Capernaum, a centurion came to Him, pleading with Him, saying, "Lord, my servant is lying at home paralyzed, dreadfully tormented." And Jesus said to him, "I will come and heal him." The centurion answered and said, "Lord, I am not worthy that You should come under my roof. But only speak a word, and my servant will be healed. For I also am a man under authority, having soldiers under me. And I say to this one, 'Go,' and he goes; and to another, 'Come,' and he comes; and to my servant, 'Do this,' and he does it." When Jesus heard it, He marveled, and said to those who followed, "Assuredly, I say to you, I have not found such great faith, not even in Israel! And I say to you that many will come from east and west, and sit down with Abraham, Isaac, and Jacob in the kingdom of heaven. But the sons of the kingdom will be cast out into outer darkness. There will be weeping and gnashing of teeth." Then Jesus said to the centurion, "Go your way; and as you have believed, so let it be done for you." And his servant was healed that same hour.

(Matthew 8:5–13)

Think about what the centurion said. He said, "You don't have to come to my house. All You have to do is speak the word and my servant will be healed." That's why so many times in a miracle service we say, "I speak the word of healing. Be healed in Jesus' name." Jesus said that all we have to do is just speak the word of healing.

Now when Jesus had come into Peter's house, He saw his wife's mother lying sick with a fever. So He touched her hand, and the fever left her. And she arose and served them. (Matthew 8:14–15)

He touched her hand. Notice that the only thing He did was to touch her. All it takes is just one touch of Jesus! Even though we think of Jesus as having ascended into heaven, remember that Jesus is here right now. As I stretch my hand to you right now, through this book, I want you to feel the touch of Jesus in your body for whatever your need might be. The Lord just gave me a word of knowledge that thousands of people are going to be healed as they read this book on healing. If you don't get your healing the first time, read it over and over until you do!

When evening had come, they brought to Him many who were demon-possessed. And He cast out the spirits with a word, and healed all who were sick.
(Matthew 8:16)

He cast out evil spirits with His Word. There is healing in the Word of God. The Scripture about the Sun of Righteousness rising with healing in His wings is for today—right now!

While He spoke these things to them, behold, a ruler came and worshiped Him, saying, "My daughter has just died, but come and lay Your hand on her and she will live." So Jesus arose and followed him, and so did His disciples. And suddenly, a woman who had a flow of blood for twelve years came from behind and touched the hem of His garment. For she said to herself, "If only I may touch His garment, I shall be made well." But Jesus turned around, and when He saw her He said, "Be of good cheer, daughter; your faith has made you well." And the woman was made well from that hour. When Jesus came into the ruler's house, and saw the flute players and the noisy crowd wailing, He said to them, "Make room, for the girl is not dead, but sleeping." And they ridiculed Him. But when the crowd was put outside, He went in and took her by the hand, and the girl arose. (Matthew 9:18–25)

Isn't that beautiful faith? Notice what happened while Jesus was on the way to the ruler's home. A woman touched the hem of Jesus' garment and was made well from that hour! She had so much faith that she said, "If I can just reach out and touch Him, if I can just touch the hem of His garment, I shall be made whole." All you need to do is to touch the hem of Jesus' garment.

Can you believe that people were laughing at Jesus when He entered the man's home? People still do that today. People who don't believe the Word of God, people who don't believe in divine healing, are laughing in the face of God just exactly the way those people laughed when Jesus told them that the girl was not dead, but sleeping.

Think of how many people you know now who laugh and say, "Healing isn't for today." Beloved, talk to the person who has been healed; he knows that it is true. Look at what happened next. Jesus sent all of the people outside. He didn't want any unbelievers in there. When active unbelief is present, it is difficult to be healed.

I know there is a gift of healing, and I praise the Lord that we have this. Charles and I see many people in our services healed by this manifestation. When things are really serious and I must pray for somebody, I ask the unbelievers to get out of the room. Why? Once again, when unbelievers are present, it can stop the healing.

Notice what happened in this case:

He said to them, "Make room, for the girl is not dead, but sleeping." And they ridiculed Him. But when the crowd was put outside, He went in and took her by the hand, and the girl arose. (Matthew 9:24–25)

When Jesus had the unbelievers removed, He went in, and the young girl arose!

I believe we see many more healings at the end of a miracle service because the unbelievers are the ones who generally get up and leave early. They are the ones who keep the miracles from happening. As soon as they leave, things begin to happen just as they did with Jesus. When the people got up and left, then the girl who was dead was brought back to life.

The Word of God reveals the following:

And the report of this went out into all that land. When Jesus departed from there, two blind men followed Him, crying out and saying, "Son of David, have mercy on us!" And when He had come into the house, the blind men came to Him. And Jesus said to them, "Do you believe that I am able to do this?" They said to Him, "Yes, Lord." Then He touched their eyes, saying, "According to your faith let it be to you." And their eyes were opened. And Jesus sternly warned them, saying, "See that no one knows it." But when they had departed, they spread the news about Him in all that country. As they went out, behold, they brought to Him a man, mute and demon-possessed. And when the demon was cast out, the mute spoke. And the multitudes marveled, saying, "It was never seen like this in Israel!" But the Pharisees said, "He casts out demons by the ruler of the demons." Then Jesus went about all the cities and villages, teaching in their synagogues, preaching the gospel of the kingdom, and healing every sickness and every disease among the people. (Matthew 9:26–35)

Note what He did first of all. He went about all the cities and villages teaching, teaching, teaching. This is one of the things that we really need today.

People need to be taught the Word of God. We need to be taught the promises of God so that we can understand what God's Word has to say about healing. He taught, He preached, and then He healed every sickness and every disease among the people. When you begin to absorb the Word of God and you begin to eat and eat and have spiritual feast after spiritual feast on every subject in the Bible, then you will be able to understand more about God's desire and ability to heal.

And when He had called His twelve disciples to Him, He gave them power over unclean spirits, to cast them out, and to heal all kinds of sickness and all kinds of disease. (Matthew 10:1)

God is not doing anything less today than He did in those days! God is calling to His people and saying, "I want you to go out, I want you to cast out devils, and I want you to heal all manner of disease."

Jesus gave this ability to His disciples, but He also gave us the power to go out. He gave them the commission to go and to heal all manner of disease, and they did! We should, too.

Now Peter and John went up together to the temple at the hour of prayer, the ninth hour. And a certain man lame from his mother's womb was carried, whom they laid daily at the gate of the temple which is called Beautiful, to ask alms from those who entered the temple; who, seeing Peter and John about to go into the temple, asked for alms. And fixing his eyes on him, with John, Peter said, "Look at us." So he gave them his attention, expecting to receive something from them. Then Peter said, "Silver and gold I do not have, but what I do have I give you: In the name of Jesus Christ of Nazareth, rise up and walk." And he took him by the right hand and lifted him up, and immediately his feet and ankle bones received strength. So he, leaping up, stood and walked and entered the temple with them; walking, leaping, and praising God. And all the people saw him walking and praising God. Then they knew that it was he who sat begging alms at the Beautiful Gate of the temple; and they were filled with wonder and amazement at what had happened to him.

(Acts 3:1–10)

Jesus had gone through this same gate over and over again. But Jesus had never healed the man who had been lying there for thirty-seven years. Jesus had walked by there many times and had not healed this man. Why? Because

He wanted to show the disciples that He had given them the power to heal and to cast out demons. The Scripture could just as well have said, "Now Charles and Frances went up together to the temple at the hour of prayer, the ninth hour." We could tell you about many people who have come out of wheelchairs just exactly the way this man did.

This man had been lame from birth. They carried him every day to the gate of the temple so that he could beg for his livelihood. Nobody had enough faith to pray that he would be healed.

And His name, through faith in His name, has made this man strong, whom you see and know. Yes, the faith which comes through Him has given him this perfect soundness in the presence of you all. (Acts 3:16)

We were in Albuquerque, New Mexico, for a seminar, and a tiny girl named Belinda was brought in during the lunchtime break. She had contracted a virus that was destroying her muscles, and she was shriveling up and dying a slow death.

A friend had called her parents and told them about our sevices, and they had brought Belinda. How we praised God we hadn't gone to lunch!

Before we prayed, Belinda looked up and said, "I have

faith in God!" We prayed and told her to get up and walk in the name of Jesus. She shot out of the wheelchair like a rocket, but crumpled to the floor because her little legs did not hold her. But we knew that she had been healed!

Charles picked her up, set her on her feet again, and said, "In Jesus' name!" This time she didn't fall down. She walked and walked and walked! She knew that the power in the name of Jesus had healed her!

Jesus, how we thank You for giving us the right and the authority to use Your name that brings healing and deliverance.

Many years ago we met a young lady named "Bobbie." Bobbie had contracted Guillian-Barre syndrome, which is an incurable disease. This is a horrible disease that atrophies and paralyzes all the muscles so that a person can no longer walk. This is not multiple sclerosis. It is Guillian-Barre. It is caused by an inflammation of the nerves. It causes the muscles to be completely destroyed.

We had met her the year before, and she had been bubbling over with the joy of the Lord. She had been excited about everything. But during the year the Devil had really hit her with this horrible disease, for which there is no known cure. As I understand it, the disease gradually progresses. It starts with the extremities and creeps upward until it causes paralysis in the lung area, and the person can no longer breathe.

Bobbie read the Word of God. She read how Peter and John had gone to the temple and had said to the lame man, whom Jesus had walked by so many times, *"In the name of Jesus Christ of Nazareth, rise up and walk"* (Acts 3:6).

When we started the service in her city, she was sitting right in the front row. She was the first one there. She said, "I want to tell you this. I just believe that when you tell me to get up and walk in the name of Jesus, I'm going to get up and walk, and I'm going to be healed."

Her faith was great! When we entered the service that night, she was the first one I saw. I had already heard about this horrible, crippling disease. I saw her on crutches. I asked her some of the symptoms of the disease and some of the things that it causes. She said, "I can't walk because if I get up, I just fall right down. There is absolutely no strength in my legs."

I prayed for her. I stood her up on her crutches. I don't remember exactly what I prayed, but at the end I said, "In the name of Jesus of Nazareth, rise up and walk," and she fell under the power of God.

Because she was unable to get up from the floor, everybody ran over to pick her up. I said, "Don't touch her! She's been healed by the power of God."

Bobbie struggled. I have never seen so much faith in my whole life. She was really putting her faith into action as she struggled and struggled, until she finally got to her feet, totally healed by the power of God! Putting her faith into action was a big key to her healing.

After that, she was walking, leaping, praising God, and saying to the whole world, "I am healed because of the power in the name of Jesus."

She said, "You may not even remember it, but when I fell under the power of God, you picked up my crutches and threw them as hard as you could into a corner. You said, 'Don't anybody give her those crutches back because she will never need them again.""*

🦟

And His name, through and by faith in His name, has made this man whom you see and recognize well and strong. [Yes] the faith which is through and by Him [Jesus] has given the man this perfect soundness [of body] before all of you. (Acts 3:16 AMP)

🦟

I get so excited because I know that the power of God has not lessened one iota!

If you are not in a wheelchair and you're not crippled, I want you to give or lend this book to somebody who is. I believe that when they read this book and read what I'm going to say right now, they will get up and walk:

🦟

Silver and gold I do not have, but what I do have I give you: In the name of Jesus Christ of Nazareth, rise up and walk. (Acts 3:6)

🦟

The Word of God is anointed today as I read it and write it down. My office is filled with the power and the presence of God. With every ounce of

*Account originally published in *How to Heal the Sick* by Charles and Frances Hunter.

belief and every ounce of faith that I have in me, I believe that if you will take this Word of God like a medicine, it will work for you. Don't just take it once and that's all. As I am instructing you by the Spirit of God, continue taking it over and over again into your very spirit, into your very being, into the innermost part of your heart. I believe you will be healed of whatever your disease may be.

Jesus gave to the disciples the power to heal all manner of disease. He has not taken that power away from people in this day and age. Look at what the Bible says:

And through the hands of the apostles many signs and wonders were done among the people. And they were all with one accord in Solomon's Porch....And believers were increasingly added to the Lord, multitudes of both men and women, so that they brought the sick out into the streets and laid them on beds and couches, that at least the shadow of Peter passing by might fall on some of them. (Acts 5:12, 14–15)

Right now, let us be in one accord! The early Christians had
so much faith, and they were all in one accord. They brought
people and laid them on the streets so that even the shadow, just
the shadow, of Peter passing by might touch some of them, and
they would be healed.

*Also a multitude gathered from the surrounding cities to Jerusalem, bringing
sick people and those who were tormented by unclean spirits, and they
were all healed.* (Acts 5:16)

God has not changed. God has promised us that someday
Charles and I will walk into an auditorium and wave our
hands, and every person in that auditorium will be
totally and completely healed by the power of God.
This will not be because of us but because of
the power of God.

Jesus has gone to heaven, but He is now living
on earth in us believers. We disciples are acting
in the power of the same Holy Spirit as the first
disciples did.

Therefore those who were scattered went everywhere preaching the word. Then Philip went down to the city of Samaria and preached Christ to them. And the multitudes with one accord heeded the things spoken by Philip, hearing and seeing the miracles which he did. For unclean spirits, crying with a loud voice, came out of many who were possessed; and many who were paralyzed and lame were healed. And there was great joy in that city. (Acts 8:4–8)

There is no faster way to make people come to Jesus than to let them see miracles.

Philip spoke, and look what happened. The unclean spirits cried and came out. There were many who were possessed; there were many who had palsy; there were many who were lame, and they were healed. Why? Because of the power of God.

There is bound to be great joy in any city when everybody gets healed. I can't wait for that day. I think that will be one of the most exciting days of my entire life. God will probably hold it off until just before the Rapture, because He knows I probably wouldn't be able to stand it if it happened before then.

*

Now it came to pass, as Peter went through all parts of the country, that he also came down to the saints who dwelt in Lydda. There he found a certain man named Aeneas, who had been bedridden eight years and was paralyzed. And Peter said to him, "Aeneas, Jesus the Christ heals you. Arise and make your bed." Then he arose immediately. So all who dwelt at Lydda and Sharon saw him and turned to the Lord. (Acts 9:32–35)

*

The man rose up immediately. Just like that! Why? Because of the power of Peter? No. Peter gave all the glory to God.

Do you see why miracles and healing will turn people to God? They did in the Bible, and the same will happen today.

At Joppa there was a certain disciple named Tabitha, which is translated Dorcas. This woman was full of good works and charitable deeds which she did. But it happened in those days that she became sick and died. When they had washed her, they laid her in an upper room. And since Lydda was near Joppa, and the disciples had heard that Peter was there, they sent two men to him, imploring him not to delay in coming to them. Then Peter arose and went with them. When he had come, they brought him to the upper room. And all the widows stood by him weeping, showing the tunics and garments which Dorcas had made while she was with them. But Peter put them all out, and knelt down and prayed. And turning to the body he said, "Tabitha, arise." And she opened her eyes, and when she saw Peter she sat up. Then he gave her his hand and lifted her up; and when he had called the saints and widows, he presented her alive. And it became known throughout all Joppa, and many believed on the Lord. (Acts:9:36–42)

Why did many believe on the Lord? Because they saw the miracle-working power of God. People will say a sinner's prayer—you can see them do that all the time—but there is nothing that will bring them to a genuinely vital relationship with Jesus faster than seeing miracles.

And in Lystra a certain man without strength in his feet was sitting, a cripple from his mother's womb, who had never walked. This man heard Paul speaking. Paul, observing him intently and seeing that he had faith to be healed, said with a loud voice, "Stand up straight on your feet!" And he leaped and walked. (Acts 14:8–10)

Paul saw a tremendous faith in this man.

I have to mention this because sometimes I think we don't know how to pray for people. Sometimes I think that if we knew just a little more about how to really heal the sick, it could help tremendously. I am reminded of a lady who was at a Full Gospel convention one time, and who was in a wheelchair. There must have been fifty people gathered around her, praying up a storm. Nothing happened. I thought, "Oh, Jesus, all they are doing is crying and saying, 'If it be Your will.' They are not really praying—really believing." When we began to sing and they disappeared to some place or another, I ran over and said the same thing Peter and James had said: *"Silver and gold I do not have, but what I do have I give you: In the name of Jesus Christ of Nazareth, rise up and walk"* (Acts 3:6). That's exactly what she did!

I think of Houghton Lake, Michigan, where there were seven people in wheelchairs, and where God spoke to me, right into my mind and heart. He said to me, "Tell those people in the wheelchairs, every one of them, to get out and walk right now in the name of Jesus." That's exactly what I said! Do you know what happened? Number one got up, then number two, then number three, then number four, then number five, then number six, and finally number seven. Hallelujah!

Recently a lady came to one of our meetings, after having had a stroke, unable to talk. Charles has a magnificent ministry with people who have had strokes. I kept saying to her throughout the seminar, "Wait, wait, wait until I catch Charles, because I want Charles to pray for you. When Charles prays for you, I know you are going to be healed." Her faith was built and built in the Lord, but she never was where Charles was until the final day! She had sat there under all kinds of teaching. Finally I said, "There's Charles. Let's go over and get Charles to pray for you."

Charles prayed a simple little prayer. I don't even know what he prayed. He probably commanded the spirit of death to come out. That is usually what he does with strokes, because one part of the brain is dead. He said to the woman, "In the name of Jesus of Nazareth, rise up and walk." She not only got up and walked, but she also began to scream and holler and carry on. You never heard anything like it in your life. Do you know what? I would have done the same thing. If I had had a stroke and was in a wheelchair, and suddenly was healed by the power of God, I would have gotten up right then and there and yelled louder than she did.

So many people think that if it happened in the Bible, that was all right, but it couldn't happen today. Oh, but it can and does happen today!

Now God worked unusual miracles by the hands of Paul, so that even handkerchiefs or aprons were brought from his body to the sick, and the diseases left them and the evil spirits went out of them. (Acts 19:11–12)

Here is a story that thrills me every time I think about it.

A lady all the way over in England heard about somebody who was healed through a prayer cloth that we had given out. She wrote to us and told us about her little grandson, who had just been born with hydrocephalus[*] and with a congenital hip defect. She wrote and asked us if we would pray and ask God to anoint a prayer cloth so that this child would be healed.

It's amazing that the power of God doesn't leave a little cloth even when it goes overseas. It went overseas, and this little baby was asleep when the grandmother got it. She took it and put it inside the baby's tiny, clenched fist.

Instantly the buildup of fluids in the brain subsided, and the boy's head was completely normal. It was either three or six weeks later when she took the child back to the clinic where she had taken him for treatment since his birth. They said to her, "This cannot be the same child that you brought before because his head is normal and there is no congenital hip defect."

---

[*]Hydrocephalus is the abnormal buildup of cerebrospinal fluid in the ventricles of the brain.

Do I believe in the healing power of God? Yes!

Do I believe that power can be transmitted through a little prayer cloth? Yes! A baby in England is walking in a perfectly normal manner today because somebody agreed with us that the same thing would happen today as happened in the days of Peter, Paul, James, and John.

In that region there was an estate of the leading citizen of the island, whose name was Publius, who received us and entertained us courteously for three days. And it happened that the father of Publius lay sick of a fever and dysentery. Paul went in to him and prayed, and he laid his hands on him and healed him. So when this was done, the rest of those on the island who had diseases also came and were healed. (Acts 28:7–9)

Now it happened on a certain day, as He [Jesus] was teaching, that there were Pharisees and teachers of the law sitting by, who had come out of every town of Galilee, Judea, and Jerusalem. And the power of the Lord was present to heal them. Then behold, men brought on a bed a man who was paralyzed, whom they sought to bring in and lay before Him. And when they could not find how they might bring him in, because of the crowd, they went up on the housetop and let him down with his bed through the tiling into the midst before Jesus. When He saw their faith, He said to him, "Man, your sins are forgiven you." And the scribes and the Pharisees began to reason, saying, "Who is this who speaks blasphemies? Who can forgive sins but God alone?" But when Jesus perceived their thoughts, He answered and said to them, "Why are you reasoning in your hearts? Which is easier, to say, 'Your sins are forgiven you,' or to say, 'Rise up and walk'? But that you may know that the Son of Man has power on earth to forgive sins"; He said to the man who was paralyzed, "I say to you, arise, take up your bed, and go to your house." Immediately he rose up before them, took up what he had been lying on, and departed to his own house, glorifying God. (Luke 5:17–25)

I believe the power of the Lord is present to heal you today!

I want you to glorify God. I am often amazed that people who are healed in a miracle service never return to express thanks to God.

Did you see what this man did? The Bible says that he glorified God.

The thief [the Devil himself] *comes only in order to steal and kill and destroy. I came that they may have and enjoy life* [not death, but life], *and have it in abundance (to the full, till it overflows). I am the Good Shepherd. The Good Shepherd risks and lays down His [own] life for the sheep.* (John 10:10–11 AMP)

He came that you might have life, not death, and enjoy it to its fullness.

Remember that when Jesus went to the cross, He was given thirty-nine stripes on His back. In one of those stripes is victory over lupus. In one of those stripes is victory over gout. In one of those stripes is victory over any disease that you may have! Every single disease that you may have is defeated—cured by the stripes on Jesus' back.

For in it the righteousness of God is revealed from faith to faith; as it is written, "The just shall live by faith." (Romans 1:17)

I want you to look at what the *Amplified Bible* has to say about faith. This is one of the most exciting texts in the world and in all the Bibles that I've read. I've never read any description of faith that blesses me like this one does.

Now faith is the assurance (the confirmation, the title deed) of the things [we] hope for, being the proof of things [we] do not see and the conviction of their reality [faith perceiving as real fact what is not revealed to the senses.] (Hebrews 11:1 AMP)

Now, when this verse mentions *"the title deed,"* it is not referring to a deed of trust. When you have a deed of trust, you don't own your home; you have a mortgage on it. A title deed means that it is all paid for. Faith is the title deed; it's all paid for.

Look at the verse again.

Now faith is the assurance (the confirmation, the title deed) of the things [we] hope for, being the proof of things [we] do not see and the conviction of their reality [faith perceiving as real fact what is not revealed to the senses].

That's faith—*"perceiving as real fact what is not revealed to the senses."*

With faith in the Father, faith in the Son, and faith in the Holy Spirit, victories are won!

All you have to do is begin to believe and let faith rise up within you. Let it begin to bubble in your stomach or wherever the faith of God bubbles in you. Just let it begin to bubble up and bubble up until you know that you know that you know that you know that healing is for you today.

My son, do not forget my law [the Word of God],
but let your heart keep my commands; for length of
days and long life and peace they will add to you.
(Proverbs 3:1–2)

That's what the Word of God has for you.
The *Amplified* version reads, *"For length*
of days and years of a life [worth

living]...." Haven't you seen people who felt that life wasn't worth living? The verse continues, *"...and tranquility [inward and outward and continuing through old age till death], these shall they add to you."*

Recently I met a lady who came to me and said, "I want to die. I have nothing left to live for." She said, "I'm sixty-one years of age. My children have grown, and life has passed me by." I looked her right in the eye and said, "Honey, I'm sixty-one. Glory to God! I think life has just started."

I feel so sorry for people who don't understand what God desires to give. God wants to give you tranquility—inward and outward peace that will continue through old age until death.

I don't know if He makes life entirely tranquil, but He certainly makes it worthwhile. I praise His name for that.

Length of days is in her [wisdom's] *right hand, in her left hand riches and honor.* (Proverbs 3:16)

Not only can you live to be old, but you can be rich as well. Glory!

🦋

She [wisdom] *is a tree of life to those who take hold of her, and happy* [blessed, fortunate] *are all who retain her.* (Proverbs 3:18)

🦋

So they [the words of God] *will be life to your soul and grace to your neck.* (Proverbs 3:22)

🦋

Keep your heart with all diligence, for out of it spring the issues of life. (Proverbs 4:23)

🦋

Keep your heart clean and pure, and see what happens to you. Be careful what you say, too!

🦋

You are snared by the words of your mouth; you are taken by the words of your mouth.
(Proverbs 6:2)

🦋

I believe with my heart and my soul that you get what you say. If you say that you're going to be sick, and if you say that you're coming down with something, you are! I guarantee you will come down with it.

130

I heard somebody say, "I'm going to come down with this terminal disease if I don't stop having pressure." Let me tell you something. That's exactly what's going to happen. We need to make a positive confession with our mouths. Your mouth can get you into more trouble than anything I know of because the Bible says you are snared with the words of your own lips!

My son, keep my words, and treasure my commands within you. Keep my commands and live, and my law as the apple of your eye. (Proverbs 7:1–2)

It's through the Word of God that you will find divine health.

Forsake foolishness and live, and go in the way of understanding. (Proverbs 9:6)

For by me [wisdom from God] *your days will be multiplied, and years of life will be added to you.* (Proverbs 9:11)

Say this aloud as you read it: "Father, because You said my days are going to be multiplied, I claim that the years of my life shall be increased."

🐝

Treasures of wickedness profit nothing, but righteousness delivers from death. (Proverbs 10:2)

🐝

"I believe it. Father, I thank You for that promise."

🐝

The mouth of the righteous is a well of life, but violence covers the mouth of the wicked. (Proverbs 10:11)

🐝

Keep saying, "Thank You, Lord. I believe You are healing me right now. Thank You, Lord. I believe I'm being healed right now. Thank You, Lord. I believe I'm being healed right now because what I say with my mouth is what I am going to get."

🐝

The labor of the righteous leads to life, the wages of the wicked to sin. (Proverbs 10:16)

🐝

If you make your riches according to the righteousness of God, it leads to life, not death.

🐝

He who keeps instruction is in the way of life. (Proverbs 10:17)

🐝

We need to be able to take instruction and correction when it is given to us. The way you heed instruction and correction makes it possible for you to speak healing to other people!

Riches do not profit in the day of wrath, but righteousness delivers from death. (Proverbs 11:4)

The fear of the LORD prolongs days, but the years of the wicked will be shortened. (Proverbs 10:27)

I praise God that the way of the Lord is strength and a stronghold of the upright, but it is destruction to the workers of iniquity.

Father, we thank You, we praise You, for the Word of God. Father, I pray that as I speak this Word to those who are sick, the word of healing will get into their very spirits. I believe, Father, in the name of Jesus. Amen.

Promises

The Word of God is loaded with promises—promises for healing, promises that you have authority to find healing in the Word of God, and just some tremendously good instructions.

❋

Blessed be the LORD, who has given rest to His people Israel, according to all that He promised. There has not failed one word of all His good promise, which He promised through His servant Moses. (1 Kings 8:56)

❋

Keep my commands and live, and my law as the apple of your eye. Bind them on your fingers; write them on the tablet of your heart. (Proverbs 7:2–3)

❋

Heaven and earth will pass away, but My words will by no means pass away. (Matthew 24:35)

❋

Many are the afflictions of the righteous, but the LORD delivers him out of them all. (Psalm 34:19)

❋

By which have been given to us exceedingly great and precious promises, that through these you may be partakers of the divine nature. (2 Peter 1:4)

For assuredly, I say to you, whoever says to this mountain, "Be removed and be cast into the sea," and does not doubt in his heart, but believes that those things he says will be done, he will have whatever he says. Therefore I say to you, whatever things you ask when you pray, believe that you receive them, and you will have them. (Mark 11:23–24)

Let us therefore come boldly to the throne of grace, that we may obtain mercy and find grace to help in time of need. (Hebrews 4:16)

But without faith it is impossible to please Him, for he who comes to God must believe that He is, and that He is a rewarder of those who diligently seek Him. (Hebrews 11:6)

Good News

A recent spiritual discussion with a pastor revealed an extremely interesting fact to us. We all know that Jesus was sent to earth to seek and to save the lost (Luke 19:10). We believe that was His main purpose for coming to earth. If that was His purpose, then why did He spend so much of His time healing the sick? This is just an extra benefit.

This pastor said he was really asking God, "Why did Jesus spend so much time healing?" The answer he got back is awesome.

Jesus knew He was going back to heaven, but He also knew that He was going to send the Holy Spirit. In this way He could live in each and every believer through the power of the Holy Spirit. Jesus wanted to live inside healthy bodies; that is why He spent so much time laying hands on the sick. He wanted them healed so that He would actually have healthy bodies to live in.

Isn't that an awesome revelation? Isn't it wonderful that His desire to live in healthy bodies was so strong that He made provision for you and me to be healed?

Jesus Is Greater than the Devil

Many people spend so much time fighting the Devil because they fail to realize that Jesus defeated the Devil 2,000 years ago!

Because of this, we don't have to spend all of our time fighting him, but we do need to remember that the Devil comes to steal, to kill, and to destroy (John 10:10)! We need to be aware of this, and we need to be reminded at all times that Jesus is much greater than the Devil. His power is much stronger than that of the Devil. This fact needs to be established in our minds once and for all.

One of the greatest Scriptures to remember is this:

He Who lives in you is greater (mightier) than he who is in the world. (1 John 4:4 AMP)

Don't ever forget that the Jesus who lives on the inside of you is greater than any power that the Devil has. All the books of the Bible contain many really good Scriptures showing how Jesus defeated the Devil.

Here is a great Scripture. It says,

For this purpose the Son of God was manifested, that He might destroy the works of the devil. (1 John 3:8)

Then the seventy returned with joy, saying, "Lord, even the demons are subject to us in Your name." (Luke 10:17)

Luke 10:19–20 shows us the fact that Jesus gave us authority over *"all the power of the enemy."* Jesus said,

Behold, I give you the authority to trample on serpents and scorpions, and over all the power of the enemy, and nothing shall by any means hurt you. Nevertheless do not rejoice in this, that the spirits are subject to you, but rather rejoice because your names are written in heaven.

Jesus Cast Out Devils

Throughout the New Testament, Jesus showed the power He had over the Devil, and He used many different ways to cast him out.

When evening had come, they brought to Him many who were demon-possessed. And He cast out the spirits with a word, and healed all who were sick. (Matthew 8:16)

We need to remember that Jesus cast out every one of the evil spirits *"with a word."* In Matthew 9 we see Jesus again displaying His power:

As they went out, behold, they brought to Him a man, mute and demon-possessed. And when the demon was cast out, the mute spoke. And the multitudes marveled, saying, "It was never seen like this in Israel!" (Matthew 9:32–33)

Looking at this Scripture, I find it amazing how casting out a devil so impressed the people. They could not get over the fact that, in their whole lives, they had never seen anything like this.

Once again the Word says, *"Then one was brought to Him who was demon-possessed, blind and mute; and He healed him, so that the blind and mute man both spoke and saw"* (Matthew 12:22).

Notice that, in each of these examples, Jesus did not spend all night casting out devils. He merely spoke the Word, knowing who He was and knowing that the power He had was sufficient, so that demons were forced to leave.

Hebrews 2:14–15 has some heartening words for all of us:

That through death He might destroy him who had the power of death, that is, the devil, and release those who through fear of death were all their lifetime subject to bondage.

Through His death He destroyed the power of the Devil and thereby released all Christians who are subject to bondage!

At evening, when the sun had set, they brought to Him all who were sick and those who were demon-possessed. And the whole city was gathered together at the door. Then He healed many who were sick with various diseases, and cast out many demons; and He did not allow the demons to speak, because they knew Him. (Mark 1:32–34)

Note that when Jesus cast the devils out, He did not allow them to talk back to Him. So don't let a demonic spirit talk back to you, either!

Luke 4:32–36 should encourage us to know that we do not have to put up with the works of the Devil.

And they were astonished at His teaching, for His word was with authority. Now in the synagogue there was a man who had a spirit of an unclean demon. And he cried out with a loud voice, saying, "Let us alone! What have we do to with You, Jesus of Nazareth? Did You come to destroy us? I know who You are; the Holy One of God!" But Jesus rebuked him, saying, "Be quiet, and come out of him!" And when the demon had thrown him in their midst, it came out of him and did not hurt him. Then they were all amazed and spoke among themselves, saying, "What a word this is! For with authority and power He commands the unclean spirits, and they come out."

We should never be amazed when we speak the Word of God and see that a devil has to go. We know that we have more power than the Devil because Jesus gave it to us; therefore, we should expect the demon to come out.

Luke 8:27–36 tells an interesting story that we need to get down into our spirits so that we will know and believe the truth about the power of God.

And when He stepped out on the land, there met Him a certain man from the city who had demons for a long time. And he wore no clothes, nor did he live in a house but in the tombs. When he saw Jesus, he cried out, fell down before Him, and with a loud voice said, "What have I to do with You, Jesus, Son of the Most High God? I beg You, do not torment me!" For He had commanded the unclean spirit to come out of the man. For it had often seized him, and he was kept under guard, bound with chains and shackles; and he broke the bonds and was driven by the demon into the wilderness. Jesus asked him, saying, "What is your name?" And he said, "Legion," because many demons had entered him. And they begged Him that He would not command them to go out into the abyss. Now a herd of many swine was feeding there on the mountain. So they begged Him that He would permit them to enter them. And He permitted them. Then the demons went out of the man and entered the swine, and the herd ran violently down the steep place into the lake and drowned. When those who fed them saw what had happened, they fled and told it in the city and in the country. Then they went out to see what had happened, and came to Jesus, and found the man from whom the demons had departed, sitting at the feet of Jesus, clothed and in his right mind. And they were afraid. They also who had seen it told them by what means he who had been demon-possessed was healed.

Luke 9:38–42 is another incredible story of the power that Jesus had and still has today.

🦋

Suddenly a man from the multitude cried out, saying, "Teacher, I implore You, look on my son, for he is my only child. And behold, a spirit seizes him, and he suddenly cries out; it convulses him so that he foams at the mouth, and it departs from him with great difficulty, bruising him. So I implored Your disciples to cast it out, but they could not." Then Jesus answered and said, "O faithless and perverse generation, how long shall I be with you and bear with you? Bring your son here." And as he was still coming, the demon threw him down and convulsed him. Then Jesus rebuked the unclean spirit, healed the child, and gave him back to his father.

🦋

Acts 10:38 is an excellent verse to put into your spirit:

🦋

God anointed Jesus of Nazareth with the Holy Spirit and with power, who went about doing good and healing all who were oppressed by the devil, for God was with Him.

🦋

Jesus Gave Us His Power over the Devil

Jesus had all power in heaven and on earth:

And Jesus came and spoke to them, saying, "All authority has been given to Me in heaven and on earth." (Matthew 28:18)

Luke 10:19 shows us that He turned around and gave His authority to us. He said,

Behold, I give you the authority to trample on serpents and scorpions, and over all the power of the enemy, and nothing shall by any means hurt you.

I am repeating this verse of Scripture because it has a second purpose here. It shows that Jesus gave *you*, the believer, that power over the Enemy.

Then He called His twelve disciples together and gave them power and authority over all demons, and to cure diseases. He sent them to preach the kingdom of God and to heal the sick. (Luke 9:1–2)

It doesn't say that He gave them a little bit of authority. It doesn't say that He gave them just enough authority so that a few demons would be cast out. It says that He gave them power and authority over each and every demon spirit. We still have authority over every demon that has ever attacked or possessed. We need to take this to heart and remember this important fact at all times!

The Great Commission of the Bible, as it appears in Mark 16:15–18, includes this truth: *"And these signs will follow those who believe"* (verse 17). In other words, every believer is going to have signs and wonders following him. The first one that Jesus mentioned was, *"In My name they will cast out demons"* (verse 17). This is so important to remember. He said that we could use His name, and that, at the very mention of His name, devils would be cast out!

Also a multitude gathered from the surrounding cities to Jerusalem, bringing sick people and those who were tormented by unclean spirits, and they were all healed. (Acts 5:16)

Acts 8:6–8 gives us another example of how Jesus gave His power to us:

And the multitudes with one accord heeded the things spoken by Philip, hearing and seeing the miracles which he did. For unclean spirits, crying with a loud voice, came out of many who were possessed; and many who were paralyzed and lame were healed. And there was great joy in that city.

Prayer Cloths Work

The world rejoices when you are healed, and that is why there was great joy in that city. That is exactly what Jesus wants.

✻

Now God worked unusual miracles by the hands of Paul, so that even handkerchiefs or aprons were brought from his body to the sick, and the diseases left them and the evil spirits went out of them. (Acts 19:11)

✻

A small piece of cloth or anything that is anointed of God and placed on a sick person can cause the evil spirits to come right out of them. Those Scriptures are just as good today as they were 2,000 years ago.

John 14:12–14 is another wonderful example of the fact that Jesus gave us authority over all the devils and demons:

✻

Most assuredly, I say to you, he who believes in Me, the works that I do he will do also; and greater works than these he will do, because I go to My Father. And whatever you ask in My name, that I will do, that the Father may be glorified in the Son. If you ask anything in My Name, I will do it.

✻

Jesus cast out devils, and so He tells us in this particular Scripture that we can do exactly the same thing, and we can do even greater things than He did. What a privilege, what a blessing, and what a responsibility!

I have written to you, young men, because you are strong, and the word of God abides in you, and you have overcome the wicked one. (1 John 2:14)

Jesus made it so plain that we have more power because He overcame the Wicked One; we have therefore overcome the Wicked One, as well!

And I will give you the keys of the kingdom of heaven, and whatever you bind on earth will be bound in heaven, and whatever you loose on earth will be loosed in heaven. (Matthew 16:19)

What power Jesus has given to us!

The Name of Jesus Is above Every Other Name

※

Therefore God also has highly exalted Him and given Him the name which is above every name, that at the name of Jesus every knee should bow, of those in heaven, and of those on earth, and of those under the earth, and that every tongue should confess that Jesus Christ is Lord, to the glory of God the Father. (Philippians 2:9–11)

※

Remember at all times that the name of Jesus has more power than the Devil ever could have. He may have thought of it, but he didn't get it!

※

Resist the devil and he will flee from you.
(James 4:7)

※

One of the things we need to remember is to resist the Devil, because that is exactly what the Bible tells us to do. The only part of the Devil that you should see is his back as he is running from you.

Be sober, be vigilant; because your adversary the devil walks about like a roaring lion, seeking whom he may devour. Resist him, steadfast in the faith, knowing that the same sufferings are experienced by your brotherhood in the world. (1 Peter 5:8–9)

The Word of God tells us to resist the Devil. It doesn't say we have to fight him all the time, but it says to resist him. Our weapons are so much better than anything the Devil has. The Bible tells us,

For the weapons of our warfare are not carnal but mighty in God for pulling down strongholds, casting down arguments and every high thing that exalts itself against the knowledge of God, bringing every thought into captivity to the obedience of Christ. (2 Corinthians 10:4–5)

Nor give place to the devil. (Ephesians 4:27)

This is a great thing to remember at all times when we are standing up against the Devil. Do not give Satan a place, or room, to live in your world.

151

Finally, my brethren, be strong in the Lord and in the power of His might. Put on the whole armor of God, that you may be able to stand against the wiles of the devil. For we do not wrestle against flesh and blood, but against principalities, against powers, against the rulers of the darkness of this age, against spiritual hosts of wickedness in the heavenly places. Therefore take up the whole armor of God, that you may be able to withstand in the evil day, and having done all, to stand. Stand therefore, having girded your waist with truth, having put on the breastplate of righteousness, and having shod your feet with the preparation of the gospel of peace; above all, taking the shield of faith with which you will be able to quench all the fiery darts of the wicked one. And take the helmet of salvation, and the sword of the Spirit, which is the word of God; praying always with all prayer and supplication in the Spirit. (Ephesians 6:10–18)

When the enemy comes in like a flood, the Spirit of the Lord will lift up a standard against him.
(Isaiah 59:19)

The Devil Is a Liar

❧

Now the serpent was more cunning than any beast of the field which the LORD *God had made. And he said to the woman, "Has God indeed said, 'You shall not eat of every tree of the garden'?"* (Genesis 3:1)

❧

We all know what happened as a result of this incident. God had spoken and said, "You can eat of every tree in the Garden of Eden, except the Tree of Knowledge of Good and Evil." (See Genesis 2:16–17.) The Devil is a liar; he came and told Eve that she could eat of the Tree of Knowledge of Good and Evil. Humanity lives out the final results of Adam and Eve's disobedience to God. Man fell, and since that time every person has been born with the sinful nature. That is why we need to remember that the Devil always creates doubt. Satan's joy in life is to try to trick you at all times.

❧

Why do you not understand My speech? Because you are not able to listen to My word. You are of your father the devil, and the desires of your father you want to do. He was a murderer from the beginning, and does not stand in the truth, because there is no truth in him. (John 8:43–44)

❧

When he speaks a lie, Satan speaks from his own resources, for he is a liar and the father of lies (verse 44).

But a certain man named Ananias, with Sapphira his wife, sold a possession. And he kept back part of the proceeds, his wife also being aware of it, and brought a certain part and laid it at the apostles' feet. But Peter said, "Ananias, why has Satan filled your heart to lie to the Holy Spirit and keep back part of the price of the land for yourself? While it remained, was it not your own? And after it was sold, was it not in your own control? Why have you conceived this thing in your heart? You have not lied to men but to God." Then Ananias, hearing these words, fell down and breathed his last. So great fear came upon all those who heard these things. (Acts 5:1–5)

This is an excellent example of how Satan would like to cause us to lie, because he is a liar and the father of lies. We need to be very careful that we know and fully understand that he is a liar and wants to make us liars, too. We must be doubly careful that we avoid any temptation to lie. He attempts to deceive the entire world. We need to be on guard and mature in faith because we have all the power we need to overcome him.

And these are the ones by the wayside where the word is sown. When they hear, Satan comes immediately and takes away the word that was sown in their hearts. (Mark 4:15)

We need to resist the Devil at all times. We must stand against him not only in sickness, but also in every other area of our lives.

Defeating the Devil

Over and over again we want to remind you to put on the whole armor of God, so that you will be able to stand against the tricks of the Devil.

Put on the whole armor of God, that you may be able to stand against the wiles of the devil. For we do not wrestle against flesh and blood, but against principalities, against powers, against the rulers of the darkness of this age, against spiritual hosts of wickedness in the heavenly places. Therefore take up the whole armor of God, that you may be able to withstand in the evil day, and having done all, to stand. (Ephesians 6:11–13)

Above all, taking the shield of faith with which you will be able to quench all the fiery darts of the wicked one. (Ephesians 6:16)

This shield of faith is something that you should never take off, even when you go to bed at night, because the Devil is right there to get in through any little crack in your armor that he can find.

But You, O L<small>ORD</small>, are a shield for me. (Psalm 3:3)

His truth shall be your shield and buckler. (Psalm 91:4)

For the word of God is living and powerful, and sharper than any two-edged sword, piercing even to the division of soul and spirit, and of joints and marrow, and is a discerner of the thoughts and intents of the heart. (Hebrews 4:12)

Keep in mind at all times that the greatest sword and the greatest shield that you could ever have is the Word of God. Get it in your spirit and keep it there.

Surely He shall deliver you from the snare of the fowler and from the perilous pestilence. (Psalm 91:3)

He has delivered us from the power of darkness and conveyed us into the kingdom of the Son of His love. (Colossians 1:13)

Praise Is Faith at Work

Praise lifts your eyes from the battle to the victory, for Christ is already the Victor. You have the Victor in your heart so that you might have His victory in your life.

Have you ever noticed the way God multiplies your faith when you begin praising Him? There are times when it is more important to praise God than to pray to Him a prayer of intercession. Praise lifts your eyes from your circumstances to your almighty Father who is Ruler over all. Not one circumstance in your life can come without His permission, and that means that He has a way of causing it to work together with other things for His glory and your good.

Again, praise lifts your eyes from the battle to the victory, for Christ is already the Victor. Though we do not yet see all things under His feet, they are there in a divine reality (Hebrews 2:8; Ephesians 1:22).

When you need faith, there are two steps to take: go to God's Word, and begin praising Him. These two go together as naturally as hydrogen and oxygen together make water. Stop worrying and fearing; try praising. Do you need faith? Praise the Lord!

If you want a new fountain of joy to spring up in your soul, start praising God. God's Word tells us that He places a song in our hearts. (See Psalm 40:3.)

If we are not singing Christians, we are disappointing God. God wants His people to begin His worship, to approach Him, with praise: *"Enter into his gates with thanksgiving, and into his courts with praise"* (Psalm 100:4). All the graces of the Holy Spirit grow much better in a happy heart.

In each crisis, when God meets the soul in a new way, He brings unspeakable joy, new peace, a touch of His glory—and praise is as inevitable as water flowing from a fountain. Whenever the clouds of darkness begin to hide God's loving face, praise is the quickest way through to His glorious light again.

Is your spiritual life lacking in joy? Be sure that there is no hidden sin, and then just start praising God. Praise the Lord!

Have you ever realized that God's answers to your prayers are at times delayed by your lack of praise to Him? Have you seen God remove insurmountable difficulties and obstructions in answer to praise? Did you know that you can often rout Satan faster by praise than by any other way? Have you experienced the effectiveness of praise and fasting? Did you know that bodies have been healed, demons have been cast out, and peace has been restored to troubled hearts simply by believers praising the Lord?

Have you ever deliberately gone into an impossible situation with the weapon of praise to God, and watched God perform the miracle? O hungry-hearted, struggling child of God, O saint of God battling the forces of darkness, O interceding prayer warrior, this may be God's message to you! Look up right now and begin to praise God. Praise the Lord!

Perhaps it is only seldom that God wants us to do nothing but ask and intercede. It may also be true that God seldom wants us to spend an extended amount of time in nothing but praise to Him. We need a healthy dose of both praise and intercession.

There is scarcely a spiritual conflict into which we enter without some measure of prayer. But how often do we, like Judah under Jehoshaphat (2 Chronicles 20:20–22), march into battle doing nothing but believing and praising? O my Christian brothers and sisters, let us begin to praise God more. Praise changes things, and praise will transform you!

There is, at times, a deep sacrifice in praise. There are times when we must praise God though tears are in our eyes. There are times when all we can say is, "Blessed be the name of the Lord." (See Job 1:21.) There is no sweeter music under heaven, there is no more fragrant perfume, than that which arises from a life of suffering that is nevertheless filled with praise.

No doubt, today you are facing situations not of your own choosing. Can you look up right now out of your personal Gethsemane and still say, "Praise the Lord"?

Praise is the language of heaven. Praise will sweeten and sanctify all that it touches. Praise will kindle a new faith. Praise will fan the sparks of your smoldering love into a flaming love for God. Praise will start the joy bells ringing in your soul; you will soon have all heaven joining in on the chorus, and you will have a little touch of heaven in your heart. Praise will pierce through the darkness, blast away long-standing obstructions, and inject terror into the heart of Satan.

We have praised God a little and occasionally; let us praise Him more and more. We have praised God in the past; let us praise

Him right now! Look up to heaven right now and praise your mighty Redeemer. Praise Him for His love and faithfulness; praise Him for His power and goodness. He is worthy of all praise; let us praise Him now! Praise the Lord!

> He is worthy to be praised;
> He is worthy to be praised;
> He's the Lord of Glory,
> The Ancient of Days;
> He is worthy to be praised.
> —Wesley Duewel

Ye that fear the Lord, praise Him.

Whoever offers praise glorifies Me; and to him who orders his conduct aright I will show the salvation of God. (Psalm 50:23)

Praise Scriptures

Therefore by Him let us continually offer the sacrifice of praise to God, that is, the fruit of our lips, giving thanks to His name. (Hebrews 13:15)

I will praise the name of God with a song, and will magnify Him with thanksgiving. (Psalm 69:30)

Oh, that men would give thanks to the LORD for His goodness, and for His wonderful works to the children of men! Let them sacrifice the sacrifices of thanksgiving, and declare His works with rejoicing. (Psalm 107:21–22)

"I create the fruit of the lips: Peace, peace to him who is far off and to him who is near," says the LORD, "and I will heal him." (Isaiah 57:19)

❧

Then he said to them, "Go your way, eat the fat, drink the sweet, and send portions to those for whom nothing is prepared; for this day is holy to our LORD. Do not sorrow, for the joy of the LORD is your strength." (Nehemiah 8:10)

❧

I will bless the LORD at all times; His praise shall continually be in my mouth. (Psalm 34:1)

❧

Praise the LORD! I will praise the LORD with my whole heart, in the assembly of the upright and in the congregation. (Psalm 111:1)

❧

Praise the LORD! Blessed is the man who fears the LORD, who delights greatly in His commandments. (Psalm 112:1)

❧

Praise God at All Times

Some of the most incredible answers to prayer have come when people were praising God. The book of Psalms, from the first chapter to the last, is a wonderful teaching of our need to learn how to praise the Lord. Many people do not take the time to go into the Bible and find all those praise Scriptures. So, we are giving you a lot of them to memorize because they will bless your life at all times. In addition to that, praise also brings healing.

One of the most outstanding stories we ever heard regarding the power of praise was about the president of a nation in Africa who was advised that the rebels were planning a coup to pull the government out from underneath him. When a coup succeeds, the president is generally imprisoned for life or killed. He was advised to get into his presidential car, drive to the airport, and get out of the country as fast as possible.

He chose to do something else. He said, "I fell on my knees, and I began to praise God." He didn't pray and ask God to protect him under the circumstances, but he praised God for what He had done in his life up until then.

He continued praising God for quite a while. Then he got up, and before long another report came in. The report said, "They are getting closer and closer!" The shots could be heard, and the bombs could be heard. Because his workers wanted to be sure that he was safe, they again encouraged him to leave the country. He said, "I fell down on my knees, and I began to praise God once again." For an hour or so he praised God, with the shots coming closer and closer and getting louder and louder all the time.

When they told him a third time that the enemy was even closer, he again fell down on his knees and praised God.

Praise Him for everything that He has done for you—and for everything that you can't even think of. Dig back into your memory and see what you can remember.

Then, the fourth time they came in, they said, "The coup failed." It did not fail because of the might and the fighting power of those who were resisting the rebels, "'*but by My Spirit,' says the* LORD" (Zechariah 4:6). Victory was won!

166

It's time to praise God. It's time to memorize Scriptures that will help you praise God and keep thankfulness in your heart at all times.

My favorite place for finding praise Scriptures is in the last seven psalms in *The Living Bible*.

David had been in very deep depression, and he was pleading with God not to turn away from him, because he said he would die without God's presence. Then came the time when he started rejoicing. When you are depressed, this is a wonderful time to praise God and worship Him for everything He has done for you.

Bless the Lord who is my immovable Rock. He gives me strength and skill in battle. He is always kind and loving to me; he is my fortress, my tower of strength and safety, my deliverer. He stands before me as a shield. He subdues my people under me. (Psalm 144:1–2 TLB)

I will praise you, my God and King, and bless your name each day and forever. Great is Jehovah! Greatly praise him! His greatness is beyond discovery! Let each generation tell its children what glorious things he does. I will meditate about your glory, splendor, majesty, and miracles. Your awe-inspiring deeds shall be on every tongue; I will proclaim your greatness. Everyone will tell about how good you are and sing about your righteousness. Jehovah is kind and merciful, slow to get angry, full of love. He is good to everyone, and his compassion is intertwined with everything he does. All living things shall thank you, Lord, and your people will bless you. They will talk together about the glory of your kingdom and mention examples of your power. They will tell about your miracles and about the majesty and glory of your reign. For your kingdom never ends. You rule generation after generation. The Lord lifts the fallen and those bent beneath their loads. The eyes of all mankind look up to you for help; you give them their food as they need it. You constantly satisfy the hunger and thirst of every living thing. The Lord is fair in everything he does and full of kindness. He is close to all who call on him sincerely. He fulfills the desires of those who reverence and trust him; he hears their cries for help and rescues them. He protects all those who love him, but destroys the wicked. I will praise the Lord and call on all men everywhere to bless his holy name forever and forever. (Psalm 145 TLB)

Praise the Lord! Yes, really praise him! I will praise him as long as I live, yes, even with my dying breath. Don't look to men for help; their greatest leaders fail; for every man must die. His breathing stops, life ends, and in a moment all he planned for himself is ended. But happy is the man who has the God of Jacob as his helper, whose hope is in the Lord his God—the God who made both earth and heaven, the seas and everything in them. He is the God who keeps every promise.

(Psalm 146:1–6 TLB)

Hallelujah! Yes, praise the Lord! How good it is to sing his praises! How delightful, and how right!

(Psalm 147:1 TLB)

He heals the brokenhearted, binding up their wounds. He counts the stars and calls them all by name. How great he is! His power is absolute! His understanding is unlimited. The Lord supports the humble, but brings the wicked into the dust. Sing out your thanks to him; sing praises to our God, accompanied by harps. He covers the heavens with clouds, sends down the showers, and makes the green grass grow in mountain pastures. He feeds the wild animals, and the young ravens cry to him for food. The speed of a horse is nothing to him. How puny is his sight is the strength of a man. But his joy is in those who reverence him, those who expect him to be loving and kind. Praise him, O Jerusalem! Praise your God, O Zion! For he has fortified your gates against all enemies and blessed your children. He sends peace across your nation and fills your barns with plenty of the finest wheat. (Psalm 147:3–14 TLB)

Praise the Lord, O heavens! Praise him from the skies! Praise him, all his angels, all the armies of heaven. Praise him, sun and moon and all you twinkling stars. Praise him, skies above. Praise him, vapors high above the clouds. Let everything he has made give praise to him. For he issued his command, and they came into being; he established them forever and forever. His orders will never be revoked.
(Psalm 148:1–6 TLB)

Hallelujah! Yes, praise the Lord! Sing him a new song. Sing his praises, all his people. (Psalm 149:1 TLB)

Praise his name with dancing, accompanied by drums and lyre. For Jehovah enjoys his people; he will save the humble. Let his people rejoice in this honor. Let them sing for joy as they lie upon their beds. Adore him, O his people! And take a double-edged sword to execute his punishment upon the nations. Bind their kings and leaders with iron chains, and execute their sentences. He is the glory of his people. Hallelujah! Praise him! (Psalm 149:3–9 TLB)

Hallelujah! Yes, praise the Lord! Praise him in his Temple and in the heavens he made with mighty power. Praise him for his mighty works. Praise his unequaled greatness. Praise him with the trumpet and with lute and harp. Praise him with the drums and dancing. Praise him with stringed instruments and horns. Praise him with the cymbals, yes, loud clanging cymbals. Let everything alive give praises to the Lord! You praise him! Hallelujah! (Psalm 150 TLB)

Nothing Is Impossible with God

Many years ago a very distraught young woman came up to us at a meeting. She was nine months pregnant at the time. She was the last one to come up in the healing line, and she began sobbing as she told me the following heartbreaking story.

This young woman said, "I'm expecting a baby, and nineteen obstetricians have told me to abort the baby because the baby does not have a stomach, does not have kidneys, and does not have lungs that could ever develop."

She continued, "I told them I was a Christian and that I absolutely could not do that because that would be killing the little life that is on the inside of me." As a last resort, she had been brought to our meeting by her sister.

We prayed a simple little prayer. I guess complicated prayers are good, but we only pray simple little ones, because we never learned how to pray complicated prayers!

We were reminded that God has a warehouse of spare parts in heaven. We fervently asked God to put into this baby the three parts that it did not have. Then we sincerely thanked Him because we believed in faith that it was done.

We were back in a neighboring town about a month or so later when the woman's aunt came running in, carrying a birth certificate signed by nineteen doctors, saying, "This is a miracle baby because he has perfect lungs, a perfect stomach, and perfect kidneys."

Let your faith rise to the heights because nothing is impossible with God!

A few years ago we were in Barbados in the West Indies. A woman was brought to our service who had been in a wheelchair for thirteen years because of multiple sclerosis. We had asked for someone who had a back problem, and the ushers brought her up on the stage. This was not exactly what we were asking for, but since she was up there we decided to go ahead and minister to her.

Many times, in foreign countries where there is a lot of witchcraft, people have become involved in it, and healing cannot take place until that spirit of witchcraft comes out of them. Thus, we commanded a spirit of witchcraft to come out of her. After we commanded that spirit to come out, we commanded the spirit of multiple sclerosis to come out, and she fell under the power of God. Two ushers tenderly picked her up. I then said the words that I always say: *"Silver and gold I do not have, but what I do have I give you: In the name of Jesus Christ of Nazareth, rise up and walk"* (Acts 3:6). Only, I didn't say *"rise up,"* since they had picked her up. I said, "Walk in the name of Jesus."

By this time Charles had taken hold of her arm and was going to assist her along with another usher, when suddenly the realization struck her that she had been healed. She hauled off and hit Charles, and said, "Let me go, NOW!" She then turned and hit the other man. As you can well imagine, they both let her go! I jumped back as far as I could possibly jump, just to see what she was going to do next.

She confidently started out across the stage, but her first steps were so wobbly that it definitely looked as if she were going to fall down and not be able to go another step! She managed to stay on her feet, even though we thought she was going to fall down after every step. Then the next step came, and she was still on her feet. We did not touch her because she had been so positive in saying, "Let me go, NOW!"

The stage was huge, and she wobbled all the way across the stage, finally sitting down on the other side. I walked over toward her but stopped about twenty feet away from her. She said, "I haven't done this for years." I did not touch her. I did not say, "I think you've walked enough for tonight." I just stood there, waiting, when suddenly she got back up again; but by this time the power of God had really gone through her. By the time she reached the center of the stage again, she was walking as normally as anyone else!

She had worked in a bank for thirteen years. The service had been filmed by the only television station on the island of Barbados. The president of the bank said, "I want a copy of that video because I want to show it twenty-four hours a day in my bank so that people will see the power of God."

We give praise to God for what He does!

God's Healing Promises

Books by Charles and Frances Hunter

A Confession a Day Keeps the Devil Away
The Angel Book
Are You Tired?
Born Again! What Do You Mean?*
Come Alive
Don't Be Afraid of Fear*
Follow Me
Go, Man, Go!
God's Answer to Fat...LOØSE IT!
God's Big "If"*
Handbook for Healing
Hang Loose with Jesus
Heart to Heart Flip Chart
Hot Line to Heaven
How to Develop Your Faith*
How to Find God's Will*
How Do You Treat My Son Jesus?
How to Heal the Sick
How to Hear God*
How to Make Your Marriage Exciting
How to Pick a Perfect Husband...or Wife
How to Receive and Maintain a Healing
How to Receive and Minister the Baptism with the Holy Spirit*
If Charles and Frances Can Do It, YOU Can Do It, Too!
If You Really Love Me...
Impossible Miracles
Let This Mind Be in You
Memorizing Made Easy*
Strength for Today
Supernatural Horizons
There Are Two Kinds Of...*
The Two Sides of a Coin
Why Should "I" Speak in Tongues?

*Indicates this is a mini-book